Praise for Nicholas Mosley

"One of the most compelling writers in the English language today."
—Joyce Carol Oates

"Mosley is the most serious and brilliant of Britain's novelists of ideas."
—*Times* (London)

"Mosley is that rare bird: an English writer whose imagination is genuinely inspired by intellectual conundrums."
—Robert Nye, *Guardian*

"Dalkey Archive has in the English writer Nicholas Mosley a throwback, a modern mastodon whose project for fiction surpasses in grandiosity that of any American writer I know."
—Tom LeClair, *Washington Post*

"Mosley is ingenious and cunning. . . . Anybody who is serious about the state of English fiction should applaud Nicholas Mosley's audacity—his skill is unquestionable."
—*Spectator*

Also by Nicholas Mosley

Fiction

Accident
Assassins
Catastrophe Practice
Children of Darkness and Light
Corruption
The Hesperides Tree
Hopeful Monsters
Imago Bird
Impossible Object
Inventing God
Judith
Meeting Place
Natalie Natalia
The Rainbearers
Serpent
Spaces of the Dark

Nonfiction

African Switchback
The Assassination of Trotsky
Beyond the Pale
Efforts at Truth
Experience and Religion
Julian Grenfell
The Life of Raymond Raynes
Rules of the Game

THE USES OF
SLIME MOULD
ESSAYS OF FOUR DECADES

NICHOLAS MOSLEY

DALKEY ARCHIVE PRESS

First edition, 2004

Library of Congress Cataloging-in-Publication Data

Mosley, Nicholas, 1923-
    The uses of slime mould : essays of four decades / Nicholas Mosley.—1st Dalkey Archive ed.
        p. cm.
    ISBN 1-56478-361-8 (cloth) — ISBN 1-56478-360-X (pbk.)
        I. Title

PR6063.O82U84 2004
824'.914—dc22

                                                        2003070081

Partially funded by grants from the Lannan Foundation and the Illinois Arts Council,
a state agency.

Dalkey Archive Press books are published by the Center for Book Culture, a nonprofit
organization located at Milner Library, Illinois State University.

www.centerforbookculture.org

Printed on permanent/durable acid-free paper and bound in Canada.

CONTENTS

Part III | Pathology and Sanity

Part IV | Philosophy and Practice

Part V | Religion

Part VI | Science, Self, God

Introduction

What's in a Name?

When a writer feels he has exhausted the ground from which his work has sprung he can still look round at the forest floor and wonder if anything might be made from the leaves and branches that have fallen there – the articles, the reviews, the unpublished bits and pieces – if nothing else, at least a bonfire. But then in the encroaching gloom he may start glancing and reading and then not so much notice the cold; might not after all the debris have some life of its own?

There is a strange organism, both vegetable and animal, that is found on the floor of the forest; it is known as slime mould. This is an unprepossessing name for something that lives and moves so mysteriously; perhaps humans have a need to be deprecating about that which against expectation has a life of its own.

At one stage of its life-cycle a slime mould consists of numerous separate amoebae which lie scattered on the forest floor. When these have exhausted the sustenance available to them they come together – there has always been within them that by which they can do this – and form a small pillar; the pillar topples over and becomes a slug; the slug sets off across the floor of the forest – it is no bigger than a grain of corn – and crawls to where there is new ground for it to feed on. When it finds such a place it stops and puts down roots; it rears up again as a mushroom with a cap on its head; its stalk grows tall and waves in the wind. After a time the head bursts, and its seeds are scattered on new ground in the forest.

This collection of occasional writings appeared to me to have some life of its own. This could not be seen much when they were being written: I myself was moving through the forest. But the presumption of the idea that I might have been in some partnership may be alleviated if the work is graced with the name of slime mould.

NICHOLAS MOSLEY
2004

THE USES OF SLIME MOULD
ESSAYS OF FOUR DECADES

Part I
Speculation

The Coming of Wit

The philosopher Karl Jaspers suggested that a turning point in history occurred around 500 B.C. – an age in which there lived Socrates, the Greek tragedians, Confucius, Lao Tse, Buddha, Zoroaster, and the central Old Testament prophets. Through the agency of such exceptional people and the interest of others in what they were saying, some change seems to have taken place in the ways in which human beings thought about themselves. The change was to do with a person's capacity for self-reflection. Whereas previously a person's view of himself and his condition seems to have been somewhat animal-like in its acceptance, after 500 B.C. a person seemed ready to ruminate upon his lot; especially upon the fact that although he was evidently part of an animal order of things, yet in this very ability to reflect upon himself he was different. Thus there entered into his conscious life not only an extra way of thinking but a contradiction: for what he had to live with was the knowledge that although in his animal part he seemed to have little autonomy, there was also a part of him that gave him the impression he had. Such speculations by Jaspers could be ignored by scholars whose business it is to demand exact evidence for historical conjectures.

Jaspers also suggested that humanity might be moving now towards another climactic period: a suggestion which could even more easily be ignored, since Jaspers was not explicit about what he thought such a change might be; and it is anyway a habit of would-be prophets to claim that the age they live in is climactic.

That there was some profound cultural and intellectual change in the world around 500 B.C. seems undeniable; not just because of the various prophets and teachers who appeared in various places at that time to try to inform men of a growth in consciousness and of ways of dealing with the contradictions inherent in it. There was also, in the Mediterranean world at least, a striking change in the works of art that depicted the ways in which human beings thought about themselves. A walk through the archaic and classical rooms of any museum containing Greek sculpture will illustrate this; those smiling, archaic figures so blindly and almost madly striding forward change, almost exactly at 500 B.C., into the bowed, dramatically tragic characters with all the cares of the world on their shoulders. These are people who have suddenly become conscious of their predicament – who perhaps know that although cruelty and suffering are endemic in the natural order of things, yet now there is some demand upon them to refuse simply to accept this nature of which they are part; perhaps to try to alter it. And yet the impression of helplessness remains. It is as if the cares of the world that have come down contain not only demands, but impossibilities.

The reason why Jaspers said so little about the further change which might now be coming upon human consciousness seems to be that although he felt the change to be something hopeful in which old impossibilities might be resolved, when he looked round on the world he could see only occasions for despair. He died in 1969, at which time evidence for despair was still powerful. But there may yet be some evidence for old impossibilities expending themselves.

Modern philosophy, it has been said, has been little more than footnotes to the work done by Socrates and Plato in the fifth century B.C. A style of philosophy was then set which was to expose everything to question – not so much with the aim of finding answers, though the style was such that these would be attempted, as with the feeling that this process of doubt and criticism was itself the virtue of philosophy. Philosophical method was to find some theory open to attack and knock it down; to see what might be set up out of the rubble, perhaps, but with the knowledge of course that this in turn could be knocked down. Philosophical behaviour in this respect resembled a game of skittles. It was as if the way in which humanity had chosen to try to deal with impossibilities presented to it around 500 B.C. – when it seemed that there were demands but no solutions – was to try to allay the anxieties induced by this predicament by ritualistic representations of it in game-playing; so that by this the predicament might seem customary.

This also, it seems to me, has been the pattern of much social and political life since 500 B.C. It was discovered then that the most suitable form of political life was one in which the participants were encouraged to take sides and to try to knock each other down – either by argument and abuse, or from time to time in wars and revolutions – for this sort of game-playing was the best way in which humans might experience the freedom that they felt they uniquely possessed. As Sartre has said, human societies only maintain their cohesion when threatened by an enemy without and the suspicion of a traitor within; like this they also have the feel of autonomy. All this seems to be the result of the need for game-playing: so long as everything in reality is open to doubt, then for reassurance it is best if the consequent prejudice and hostility are held within the style of games.

Recently however the impression has been growing – and it is here that there might be some evidence for Jaspers's feeling of a move away from despair – that although for thousands of years there has been the idea that human consciousness functions properly if everything put up is there to be knocked down (with the exception of religious feeling perhaps; though religious people for the most part seem to like knocking each other down) yet this idea itself – that everything is open to doubt – is itself not open to doubt; and this certainty – that it is not doubtful that everything is open to doubt – is somehow cheering; in spite of (or perhaps because of) the riddle-like form in which it is put. Philosophers are notoriously wary of such statements because they go round and round; they reflect back on themselves, and do not produce a knock-down argument. They are like the statements of that enigmatic fellow, the Cretan who said that all men were liars. So was or was not the Cretan a liar? The difficulty with such statements, philosophers say, is that they transfer a statement from one logical category to another – to one that refers not just to things outside it but also to itself. And so such statements do not knock other statements down; they bend back, to their own cause and effect. The Cretan, certainly, seems less suited to a syllogism than to a limerick. And did not Plato want to ban all poets from his Republic?

In political life there seems to have arisen the idea that although the best system of government is one that is there simply to correct the abuses inherent in any system of government, yet this system, if working correctly, cannot be said to contain abuses; it has placed itself, as it were, in a different logical category. In ethics, there seems to be the growing idea that the best way of encouraging morality might be to tell people that within necessary and agreed social and legal limits they can do what they like; in this way they can learn what is likeable and what is not, whereas imposition is apt to be counter-productive, since it encourages not learning but the taking of sides. All these ideas are riddle-like, bending back on themselves; not flouting reason, but using it in complex logical categories.

I think there is evidence now that consciousness itself – the ways in which human beings see themselves and their condition – might be said to be ready to move into the acceptance of some more complex category: that whereas in 500 B.C. human beings became used to seeing themselves, which caused them some despair, now they might be said to be becoming used to seeing themselves seeing themselves; which might cause them some cheer.

There is, first, the growing realisation that the old ways of belligerent game-playing have become too dangerous: if mankind is to continue to exist, there has to be some change from the habit of national and international skittles. The change has been caused by elaboration of technology; a response is called for in the mind. The vision that might come about is that the players are in a higher category than that of the game: if players can become accustomed to seeing themselves as players as well as to being accustomed to seeing the requirements of the game, then they will see, in spite of the different sides that are necessary for games, that they as humans have some unity: and it is this that might give them encouragement for the means of staying alive. Also, of course, their games might continue: the hope, as has been said, lies not in simplicity but in complexity: old habits are not expunged; they can be superseded.

Thus in a society, for instance, if a trade union leader can see himself as a trade union leader, a capitalist as a capitalist, a materialist as a materialist and a person with a vision of God as a person with a vision of God – then, insofar as they all can thus not only see themselves but, becoming accustomed to this, see each other seeing themselves, on this ground they can meet; for they will be engaged in the same business – that of being on the level of a different category of vision, where people who are different-seeming on a lower level are the same on this higher level. They might even see themselves as slightly funny. And because they will be on this common ground they will know that damage done to one may come back to haunt another; and thus there might be harmony if not exactly peace. Man has hitherto believed himself to be a social animal: but he has only achieved this state, as Sartre said, at a terrible cost. A man cannot be a true social animal – cannot exist, that is, without taking sides – until he has been able to stand back and see himself; see himself in company with others being able to see themselves; thus exorcising the enemy without and the potential traitor within, because he will see that the need for these has been within the part of himself he can grow beyond.

A person does not easily come to terms with new visions and new attitudes unless he or she has models on which to base such understanding. In 500 B.C. there were prophets scattered around the world to exhort humans how to bear the impossible vision of themselves; now there do not seem to be many prophets to encourage a possible relationship with such apparent impossibility. Modern artists have felt the force of everything being open to question; but they have portrayed more the crippling anxiety of the question-mark rather than the fecundity of that androgynous hieroglyph bending round upon itself. If the vision of hope in the modern world is that of people becoming accustomed not only to seeing themselves and their absurdities but to others being accustomed thus to seeing themselves from this higher category of vision, then it is likely that its form of expression, referring both to what it refers to and also to itself, will be less like that of old prophets offering solace and instruction than that of the Cretan who was something of a wit.

Spectator, 1978

Runaway Mankind

Mind and Nature. By Gregory Bateson

Gregory Bateson has just died at the age of 76. When he came to lecture at the ICA last October all tickets had been sold weeks in advance. Devotees at the lecture – a hard-headed lot of scientists, psychiatrists, and so on – seemed almost reverential in the face of what he had to say. Yet Bateson is still little known in his native country (he went in his twenties to live and to work in the USA). The reason for the excitement his thought causes, together with his comparative lack of notoriety, is, it seems to me, not just the difficulty attendant on any original thinker, but the fact that his message is to do with the riddles that are the style of truthful communication.

Bateson was born in 1904 into a family of Cambridge scientists. He himself was an anthropologist, a psychologist, an ecologist, a student of cybernetics. He worked with schizophrenics and with dolphins. He is best known perhaps for his 'double-bind' theory about the role of family tensions in schizophrenia, when contradictory messages given by parents can damage children. He published one anthropological work in the '30s, *Narven*; and in 1972 a collection of his papers from journals entitled *Steps Towards an Ecology of Mind*. It was this book that won him his devotees. He recently published *Mind and Nature*, which, like its predecessor, seems to me a key book of the twentieth century.

Bateson's writing is tight-packed, erudite, allusive, witty. It is difficult to summarize him. His message is something like this.

There is a distortion at the moment in the way in which most human beings see themselves and the world. We have come to think of 'nature' as crude and materialistic; and thus, in spite of temptation to the contrary, to think of humans, being part of nature, as crude and materialistic too. But in fact what is essential about nature is its intricacy, its aestheticism, its complexity, its elegance; and it is in their possessing such qualities as these that humans are part of nature.

What people imagine to be crude and materialistic about themselves is, in fact, unnatural.

What is aesthetic about nature is that phenomena are not just disconnected instances but that they form patterns; there are hierarchies of these patterns, and of the abilities to observe patterning which themselves form patterns. What is aesthetic about human beings is not just that they are parts of nature bodily, but they have the ability to see and form connections and thus to create a patterning on a higher level. This is an ability of mind: but the whole patterning-system of nature seems to be an ability of mind.

What is common to natural and mental processes is that living things evolve not through a linear development of cause and effect but through relationship, interplay. In the evolution of living systems there are two components at work – on the one hand the random element of chance, and on the other a selective process which determines that only certain outcomes of randomness are allowed to endure. This system of interplay is called 'stochastic'.

The evolution of organisms is stochastic: the interaction between genetic endowment and forces of environment determines whether or not an organism survives. It is also thus with ideas, which survive when they are suited to what circumstances demand. But in order for such an idea about interplay to survive – as opposed to ideas about simple linear 'cause and effect' – there is required an ability for observation and for learning in the manner of what Bateson calls a 'higher logical type'. This is a phrase borrowed from logicians, who talk of a 'class' of things being a 'higher logical type' than that of its members.

The story that Bateson tells to illustrate this phrase is that of a dolphin he worked with which had been trained to perform simple tricks – to jump with a flick of its tail to the right or to the left for instance – according to a system of rewards. Such tricks were quite easy for the dolphin to learn. Then an experiment was attempted in which, each time the dolphin came into the demonstration pool, it was to be rewarded not for doing this or that particular trick, but for doing each time something new. This was a requirement, to do with an abstraction, of a higher logical type. The effort to discover this caused the dolphin some distress; then, after fourteen bewildered attempts, it learned; it came into the demonstration pool and with much enthusiasm and excitement (this is important) did a series of leaps all of which were new. What the dolphin had learned was not just a trick, but an attitude to tricks. It had succeeded – with a struggle but in the end joyfully – in an act of learning of a higher logical type.

What is necessary for human beings today, Bateson suggests, is some such learning; if there is not this learning, then societies, and the species, may simply blow themselves up. Simple 'cause-and-effect' tendencies can of course for a time be conducive to the welfare of a society; but there is no simple tendency which, if taken to excess, does not become harmful. At the moment there is an attitude in Western societies which insists that 'more' is 'better' – with regard to armaments, money, possessions, power and so on. With such an attitude society is like a steam-engine without a governor; the machinery has got into a 'runaway' situation in which it is simply likely to go faster and faster until it explodes. (Cancer is medically an example of a 'runaway' situation: it is a process in which cellular growth has lost the mechanism which tells it when to stop.) At the moment human beings seem set upon lines of simple increase of quantity: they lack aptitudes for balance, for aestheticism, for adaptation, for alternation, for control. These would be abilities of a higher logical type.

One of the genetic endowments of persons and populations is a potentiality for change: one does not have to wait for a chance mutation to encourage a different kind of learning. Myriad potentialities exist: but the forces of selection, in the minds of persons at least, are largely, though not wholly, dominated by tradition. At the moment, humans seem hidebound in various runaway ideas; a capitalist is a capitalist, a trade unionist is a trade unionist; each challenges the other and spurs the other on until a condition of breakdown is reached. What is necessary if systems are to be balanced in liveliness as opposed to flogged to death, is the encouragement of states of mind which will think naturally in terms of aestheticism rather than quantity, alternation rather than 'runaway', questioning rather than dogma. It is difficult for a human being to choose to think against tradition, but not impossible.

At the end of this book, Bateson writes simply of the necessity of an aptitude for beauty, and for the sacred. Beauty is a word to describe that which exists by virtue of relationships and pattern; sacred is a word to describe the fact that this aptitude for beauty is not something that can be encapsulated and passed on in easy words. But it is something that each person can learn for himself, with effort, when necessary. This is why Gregory Bateson will remain a sage and not a pop-guru.

Listener, 1980

Nietzsche and Creation

Nietzsche: A Critical Life. By Ronald Hayman

The merit of this well-researched book is that it never loses sight of the questions that were of central importance to Nietzsche – (in Ronald Hayman's words) 'If we lose faith in language and truth, how are we to communicate? If we lose faith in the coherence of the self, how can we expect to think coherently?' Nietzsche believed that we had in fact lost these faiths, though we tried (perhaps for the time being necessarily) to cover up the lack of them with trivial or lugubrious rituals and superstitions. But Nietzsche's life was dedicated to trying to find ways of talking, thinking and indeed of just surviving which would enable a few people in the future to face this predicament without illusion and with energy. The catch-phrases that have become associated with Nietzsche's name – the Superman, the Will to Power, and so on – have to be seen in the light of this central effort: if they are not (as too often happens) they give a perverted view of Nietzsche as some precursor of romantic totalitarianism; which perversion he himself would have hated and in fact foresaw – both the historical occurrence, and the fact that people like him would be blamed for it, as the revenge of those who depend upon illusions upon those who do not.

What seems to me a weakness of the book is that having seen so clearly the central predicament, Ronald Hayman spends too much time in describing the weird and desperate cost to Nietzsche of his attempts to deal with it – his illnesses, his loneliness, the ambiguities of much of what he wrote. What is felt only obscurely in this book is Nietzsche's amazing success; though Ronald Hayman is moved (as commentators on Nietzsche nearly always are in spite of their bafflements) to describe him as 'one of the great liberators', and to suggest that his influence on this century has been equalled only by that of Marx or Freud. But then, Nietzsche's success was such that it was not averse to bafflement.

What Nietzsche saw was that all philosophical systems, all morali-
ties, all sets of customary attitudes to life, were the outcomes not of
objective enquiry into 'truth', but rather of a person's (or a people's)
driving need for status, for self-preservation, for a feeling of identity.
Nietzsche called this the 'will to power'; and he saw it as a basic drive
of all life. But a human being had by some chance of evolution also
been landed with consciousness and a conscience; and these made
it difficult for him to admit freely that his life was dominated by a
will to power; and so he made up theories about how he was acting
according to the dictates of truth, or God, or altruism, or whatever;
and by doing this he achieved – a more acceptable sense of power!
It was this that had once been necessary for men's survival (how else
could the conflict between instinct and consciousness be borne?) but
now, in the course of time, the tension between man's predicament
and his pretences had ceased to be fruitful; and he was faced with
decadence and destruction if some new accommodation were not
made. A new type of man had to emerge ('superman') who would
be able to face with equanimity the facts of 'will to power' – and by
doing this, in fact, be able in some sense to overcome it – for what he
would then be interested in would be not the overcoming of others,
but the overcoming of himself. Ronald Hayman writes 'Nietzsche was
not immune to the desire for power, but it was for power over himself
that he lusted'. But then – what would be the mark of the new type
of man with this power-over-self? and how would its manifestations
differ from other forms of will-to-power?

It is here, it seems to me, that nearly all critics of Nietzsche lose
their way; they find themselves out of the maze and in a desert. The
thread that they have not followed is the fact that when Nietzsche
says that old forms of language are not to be trusted, what he is doing from then on is trying to use language in a new sort of way; and
if critics imagine he is not (which they usually seem to be doing) it
is then they are lost. In the old style, language is used as a protection, a justification, a defence, an attack: what are called 'truths'
are in fact (in Nietzsche's words) 'a mobile army of metaphors,
metonyms, anthropomorphisms . . . are illusions whose illusoriness
is overlooked'. But then, what is the new style of language in which
Nietzsche is writing if he is not to be caught in the trap of trying to
establish some old-fashioned argument? It seems to me that what he
is doing is to say – But once we *know* that language is used in this
way, then, in some sense, we are not using it in this way; because
our very knowledge (if we can hold it and make it felt in the style)
makes language into a sort of game, an art-work, a creation; and

what can be truly 'true' about it is just the shared knowledge that this is so; though it is this perhaps that is impossible to put directly into words. The mark of such a language would be not so much its reasonableness as its wittiness, its allusiveness, its playfulness, its irony; perhaps even its secrecy; the validity of it would be aesthetic; its potency would lie in paradoxes such as that of the Cretan who said 'All Cretans are liars' – but at least he was someone with the wit to be at home with riddles, which are what life is about. The style of people who did not want power over others but over themselves and their creations would be something like

> this secret self-ravishment, this artistic cruelty, this lust to impose a form on oneself as a tough, resistant, suffering material, cauterising into oneself a will, a criticism, a contradiction, a contempt, a negation; this uncanny, weirdly enjoyable labour of a voluntarily divided soul making itself suffer out of a pleasure in causing suffering; finally this whole, *active* 'bad conscience' – you can guess already – as the true womb of all ideal and imaginative experience.

This is the style and message of Nietzsche – from *On the Genealogy of Morals*.

Ronald Hayman is illuminating about Nietzsche's self-imposed sufferings; he sees not only their severity but what might have been their point – they gave to Nietzsche the chance to concentrate on little else but his work. Hayman also casts as much light as probably can be cast on Nietzsche's madness (he was incapacitated from the age of forty-four till his death at fifty-five in 1900): this might have been due to hereditary syphilis or to an infection picked up when young, but just as likely was to do with mental and physical strain or even a relief from it. Nietzsche had written in his youth of what seemed to him the necessity for those who 'break the yoke of a convention and make new laws' eventually to go mad or to feign madness; and some of his old friends, when they saw him after his breakdown, felt that he was pretending. But then, as Nietzsche might aphoristically have said – what is madness except the necessity to feign madness?

But to turn from the account of the lonely, half-frozen man with his blinding headaches in his cheap hotel rooms in Nice or Sils Maria to, for instance, the exuberant energy of the opening sections of *Beyond Good and Evil* is to turn from – what? – the shrieks of the chisel against the stone when the sculptor bangs away at it to the view of the marvellous sculpture itself when one stands back – and with the knowledge that these two forms of experience are part of the same creative occurrence. For what Nietzsche was trying to say finally was that this paradoxical creative process cannot be explained or justified rationally but it can be known – and it can be communicated that it is known – in some sort of life-giving style that will be a reflection of the liveliness that is otherwise beyond the terms of language. People may be deceivers, yes; but how wonderful to be a creator of deceptions! and to be aware of this! so this is not a deception. What is true about a person is just that he knows he can create; and this he can hold on to, to survive, and perhaps this need not send him mad. Unless, that is, he has continued to try to talk too much perhaps about all the things that cannot easily be talked about; and has not spent quite enough time in doing the things that are all too pleasantly talked about – such as gardening, or being with children, or making love.

Time and Tide, 1987

Not What the Doctor Ordered

Why Freud Was Wrong: Sin, Science and Psychoanalysis.
By Richard Webster

Much of the material in this interesting book has been noted before, although perhaps not so lucidly and forcefully. The thesis is: what Freud promulgated was not science but pseudoscience; he constructed hypotheses on almost no evidence, he fudged what evidence there was to fit his theories, he controlled his disciples with a revivalist fervour that exhibited the neurotic symptoms his methods were aimed to cure. All this is now largely accepted. What has also been accepted is that Freud was a prophetic innovator who opened up to healthy inquiry areas that had hitherto been shrouded.

It is this latter supposition that Richard Webster seeks to discount – first by showing that many of Freud's early ideas were not original, then by arguing that the tradition within which Freud worked has led to a dead end; and that a chance was missed to promote some real, rather than pseudo, science.

At the base of the Freudian structure was the theory of infantile sexuality: the idea that children are born with driving impulses to devour and possess; that the task of growing up is to recognise these and to learn how to sublimate them. This, Webster suggests, was within the tradition of the Christian doctrine of original sin – the belief that the impulses of the body have to be conquered by the spirit. It was also in line with a rationalist belief since the time of Descartes that in humans there is a split between mind and body; that what is possible to aspire to is mental and rational purity.

Freud imagined that he was opening windows on to stuffy religious or rationalist confinement; in fact he was adding to the tendency to see natural inclinations as unsavoury disturbances to be cured. The fact that so few of his patients were in any lasting sense cured then led him to state that the business of curing was not the point;

the point of the psychoanalytic movement was to propagate 'truth' – that is, his increasingly messianic theories based on uncorroborated evidence.

The chance that was missed at the birth of psychoanalysis, Webster suggests, was that of finding a truly scientific approach to the understanding of human personality – not using the mind to try to exorcise the nature of the body, but accepting mind and body as inseparably interacting modes of one being. For this a Darwinian approach would be needed – recognising that humans are instinctive animals engaged in evolving within them forms by which they might survive, and discovering their ecological pattern outside. In the course of this process systems of language, imagination, self-reflection and morality have evolved which indeed have made it possible for humans to survive. But if the instincts are seen as an enemy, then how much longer can the human species, at war within itself, be expected to survive?

This is a long book and there are lengthy digressions – on Charcot and hypnotism, on Levi-Strauss and structuralism, on Anna Freud. These are fascinating in themselves: but the main thesis is of such importance that one hopes it will not be missed. In an afterword Webster brings the questions at issue to the present, with an appraisal of the recent alarm concerning child abuse or, alternatively, what has been called 'false memory syndrome'.

Freud, as is now well known, at first attributed the cause of 'hysteria' in his women patients to abuse by their fathers when they were children. He later retracted, and decreed that the situations and accusations arose from his patients' fantasies. Latterly it has been suggested that his first view was correct and that he retracted out of fear of social outrage and in order to get backing for his theories about the power of fantasies. But there is also evidence, Webster claims, that it was Freud himself who pressed ideas of actual abuse on to his patients in the first place – before he realised what was needed for his theories.

The confusion has re-arisen nowadays in a virulent form, with patients under therapy claiming to remember how they were abused as children, and parents accusing therapists of implanting false memories for their own neurotic reasons. In the welter of accusation and counter-accusation the chance of discovering what actually happened is lost; as well as any chance of helping distraught patients and families.

A truly scientific approach would be that of testing how best to deal with whatever are the actual symptoms – not sacrificing sense and health to fears and doctrinaire obsessions. Actual abuse is traumatic; but some abuse, actual or conjectured, is not so traumatic as the temptation to cling to it or suggest it for self-justification. The point about original sin is that, if it can be redeemed, it has not much mattered.

Daily Telegraph, 1996

The Heart of a Venomous Squabble

A Most Dangerous Method: The Story of Jung, Freud, and Sabina Spielrein. By John Kerr

Sabina Spielrein was Jung's first psychoanalytic patient. She was an eighteen-year-old from Russia who came to his Zurich clinic in 1904 as a severe case of 'psychotic hysteria'. Within two months she was ostensibly cured – Jung having uncovered and healed the traumas caused by her experience of being beaten by her father. But what was the secret of this apparently miraculous cure?

A few years later it transpired that at the time she was having an affair with Jung; he had become as obsessed by her as she was by him. In some confusion Spielrein wrote to Freud for counsel. Freud, at that time still on the best of terms with Jung, told him of Spielrein's letter. Jung, shamefully, denied the sexual affair with his patient and made out that Spielrein was still mentally disturbed. Freud took all this coolly: it was important that there should be no scandal; Jung was vital to him in getting his psychoanalytic movement more widely recognised.

John Kerr has written a detailed and enthralling book making use of Spielrein's papers, most of which have only just been discovered. The story covers old ground in its account of the venomous squabbling that bedevilled the early years of the psychoanalytic movement; what is new is information about the great influence Spielrein had, not only on Jung and his theories, but also on an aspect of the style of Freud's movement as it evolved.

Freud had picked Jung as his 'son and heir'. As Jung grew away from him – objecting to Freud's insistence that the origins of neuroses were exclusively sexual – Freud could hint that of course there were reasons why Jung wanted to deny the power of the sexual and go off into occult mumbo-jumbo. But the latter knew, or felt he knew, another guilty secret: that Freud was involved in an incestuous relationship with his own sister-in-law. Jung was contemptuous of Freud's refusal to talk about this on the grounds that it would undermine his authority.

Against such a murky background, John Kerr claims, the psycho-analytic movement went somewhat off the rails:

> The sexual, the religious, the theoretical, became hopelessly intertwined, and they [Freud and Jung] could no longer talk about them. Not to each other and not to anyone else.

Sabina Spielrein was a far more interesting character however than just a catalyst in the split between Freud and Jung. She became a practising analyst herself and in 1911 published a paper 'Destruc-tion as a Cause of Coming into Being' which, if her colleagues had given time to reading it rather than using it as ammunition in their squabbles, might have pointed to a road along which Freud and Jung could have travelled together.

Spielrein's theory was that in order to explain neuroses and sexual difficulties it was not necessary to invent, as Freud did, bizarre hypoth-eses concerning Oedipal traumas: there was a built-in conflict in the nature of sex anyway – between the ego's instinct for self-preservation, and the instinct of the unconscious for species-preservation within which the needs of the ego were often ignored. Because of this, there was the likelihood of repression and destruction; but also the chance, if all this were recognised, of transformation and rebirth. And by seeing this comparatively simple pattern Jung's more outlandish flights into myth might also have been avoided.

The break between Jung and Freud came in 1912. Spielrein con-tinued to keep in touch with both of them; there was a plan for her to be further analysed by Freud. But then the war came, and after it Spielrein returned to Russia. About her later history little is clear, except that she married, had a child, and was shot by the Nazis in 1941 along with the other Jews of Rostov-on-Don.

Indeed, almost nothing was known of her at all except from veiled references in the Freud-Jung letters until a cache of her papers was found in Geneva in 1977, followed by two more discoveries of papers in private hands. From this John Kerr has extracted his fascinating story.

Sabina Spielrein emerges as a still small voice of much endurance and integrity perhaps destined to be swamped in battles fought with Freud's waspish skill and Jung's turgid intensity. But here she takes her place as the original model for Jung's 'anima' – that archetypal feminine force by which men unconsciously are so often held in thrall. And she seems to have been at the centre of the drama which determined that practitioners of 'the talking cure' were apt to retreat towards dogma – having found there were things about themselves of which they could not talk at all.

Daily Telegraph, 1994

Trust Life to Work with You

Life and How to Survive. By Robin Skynner and John Cleese

Ten years ago Robin Skynner and John Cleese wrote *Families and How to Survive Them.* This was a brilliant distillation of the results of 100 years of psychoanalytic and psychotherapeutic research, taking these out of the area of ponderous jargon and putting them into a light-hearted but compelling form in which any intelligent person could be encouraged to respect them. Now, in *Life and How to Survive It,* Skynner and Cleese expand on their themes and push these into areas of business, politics, society.

The message in *Families* was: the fact that humans have dark and difficult emotions is inescapable and thus in a sense it is not a problem: it is the frequent denial by humans that they have such emotions which does damage that is preventable. Conflicts within families, that is, can begin to be dealt with once these emotions are seen for what they are. Compromises can be worked out, lines of demarcation drawn. It is ignorance of one's own nature, and the projection of blame for all difficulties on to others, that result in disastrous collisions and blockages. In order to see others clearly, and to understand relationships, we have to look at ourselves.

It was recognised in *Families* that there was something slightly magical in this suggestion: how should it be that just by facing a problem, its malignancy might begin to disappear? It was implied that in experience there was a connection between the workings of the human psyche and the workings of the outside world – a connection through which, if there were efforts at recognition, healing might occur.

In their latest book this becomes the most striking vision. Robin Skynner, acting as guru, propounds his ideas about the road from sickness to health – within individuals, within the various groupings of society. Most persons and institutions have some built-in incapacities; but, if these are recognised, it is natural that they should improve. John Cleese, acting as cross-examiner, asks the vital questions: yes, but how are these recognised? Is there not a Catch-22 here? – unhealthiness being precisely the condition of being unable to see it for what it is. Skynner replies: yes, but if you expose yourself to realities, then life will do the job for you; the first step is difficult, but the chance is always there.

We have maps in our minds, that is, of how we perceive reality; we have to check these against what in fact is there. If there is a discrepancy, then it is the map that we will have to readjust. Reality will help us to do this. And then we will see more of what is there. This process can be seen as scientific.

In the final section of *Life* Skynner and Cleese become explicitly religious – not in the sense suggested by established churches and dogma, but in the sense that if one trusts that there are healing connections between the human psyche and the outside world, then this trust is in a framework that can properly be called religious – a framework within which, despite disasters and suffering, the universe can be seen to have meaning, and some process of redemption can in fact have a chance to take place. This is difficult to put into words – words have to do with the formation of maps; the appreciation of reality has more to do with watching and listening.

These are enormously important books. No literate person will any longer have an excuse to turn his or her back on psychotherapeutic evidence because of the jargon. Skynner is a rare guru because he is in no way apologetic for the grandness of his vision, yet at the same time he never loses sight (this is part of the vision after all) of his own often laughable dependency. Cleese becomes more than an expert feed-man: in the sections about politics and society he often holds the floor, and his diatribes against politicians, though simplistic, usually hit nails on the head. And there is Skynner to tell him – Yes, but societies, like individuals, can only see their idiocies, and thus progress, inch by inch.

Much of the evidence collected here has been sifted by researchers working in everyday life with families, businesses, societies, observing what can be called healthy and what can not. It is Skynner's and Cleese's hope that people may begin to pay attention to what they are saying simply because they will find that it works – persons may become in this way not only happier but materially better off. And it will be seen that people who remain in conflict and frustration often do so because in a sense this is easier and they choose to. Thus the differentiation between sheep and goats may be seen to depend on courage – the sheep are those who have the energy to look at things as they are; the goats are those who feel safer tethered to their small circles of passion and illusion.

Daily Telegraph, 1993

The Value of the Clown

R. D. Laing: A Personal View. By Bob Mullan

R. D. Laing became famous in the '60s for writing books suggesting that madness was connected to unacknowledged destructive tendencies within families – coldness and anger trying to disguise themselves as love. Later he spoke of the damage done to individuals by the contradictory messages put out by society as a whole – for instance 'love your neighbour' but 'at all costs be more successful'. Towards the end his life he claimed that humans were thrown into an impossible situation just by being born – the traumas of leaving the womb, of the cutting of the umbilical cord, causing distress that made later disturbance inevitable.

Such ideas were welcomed in the '60s and '70s when theoretical justification was needed for an instinctive revolt against family dependency that had become stultifying. *The Divided Self* and *The Politics of Experience* were seminal books through which people recognised the truth of much of what Laing was saying from their own hitherto unacknowledged experience. For the last twenty years however, Laing's reputation (he died in 1989) has fallen into disrepute; it has come to be seen that most traditional families, however confusing, are better than nothing. And anyway Laing did not say much about what in practice could be done about his bleak view of things.

He did his first work as a doctor in the '50s with psychotics – severely distressed patients in asylums in Glasgow and London. He was horrified by the coldness and brutality with which patients were treated: he determined to show them respect by trying to understand and take seriously whatever might be their delusions. He had the theory that schizophrenics were forced to construct a fantasy world to protect themselves against a mad world around them. He could personally help them by listening to them and not having contempt for their behaviour. Like this their pain was alleviated, but their state of alienation was probably not much altered.

Bob Mullan calls his book on Laing 'A Personal View' and so it is – not a biography but a tribute in sympathy with Laing, whom he was friends with in Laing's later years. Each man had had a similar difficult family background of the kind Laing wrote about. Mullan, by profession a writer and maker of documentary films, himself had psychotic spells for which the conventional treatment he received seemed irrelevant. Mullan thinks that the three biographies hitherto published about Laing also missed the point – they appreciate his early writings, but suggest that his drinking, drug-taking, erratic be-haviour and marital infidelities vitiated much of his work and teach-ing. Mullan's claim is that Laing's passionate and wayward protests against conventionality were part of his gift and charisma – his very self-destructiveness was a demonstration and thus possibly an easing of the terrible predicaments in which humans found themselves.

Mullan seems at times to vitiate his own book by bringing in too much of himself – his parents' history; his own crack-up and hospi-talisation. But this is within the style of Laing himself. Laing was a life-giver not just as a sympathiser or theorist, but as a poet, a clown. He put on a show; and in response people might learn to do what they could for themselves.

The most telling criticism of Laing (and by implication of Mullan) was made by Colin Wilson, who is quoted not in this book but in the biography of Laing by John Clay. Wilson saw Laing as an enemy because he made destructiveness and self-destructiveness appear romantic: the trickster-outsider permanently at odds with the world became a hero, and those who struggled painstakingly to cope with the world became boringly 'square'. And the dismal legacy of harping on defeat is evident in much literature and media-business today.

Mullan's book is not aimed to give an objective view of Laing. But its very subjectivity does say something interesting about not only the coldness of conventionality but the sadness of those who over-expose themselves to crack-up. Perhaps a lesson to be leaned is that if one does try to sort out oneself and other people (and family therapists have learned much in the last twenty years) it is perhaps best not to proclaim what one is doing too loudly.

Daily Telegraph, 1999

Do Humans Desire Happiness?

A lifetime of happiness! No man alive could bear it.
It would be hell on earth.

Bernard Shaw, *Man and Superman*

It was Aristotle who formulated the idea that human beings desired happiness. He argued in the logical way of the Greeks, without paying too much attention to experience, that there must be some aim to human life and that this, as a matter of definition, should be called happiness. 'Happiness, then, is something final and self-sufficient, and is the end of action'. From this point on, of course, the word and the idea could be hedged around by as many qualifications as anyone liked. Aristotle argued that perhaps no man could properly be called happy until he was dead: but then, according to the Greek tragedians, what a man might properly desire was to be dead. Logic and definitions took precedence over experience; and people were saddled with the idea that happiness was what they desired even if what for the most part they seemed to achieve was being miserable.

Later ages have not always been so obsessed by the need for definitions as were the Greeks: but the idea that as a matter of common sense human beings desire happiness has remained. It has become such a truism that when a self-conscious merchant of paradoxes such as Bernard Shaw said that if human beings ever got a lifetime of happiness they would find it hell on earth, the remark could be taken as just one of those witticisms by which platitudes are stood on their heads. It is only if one gives oneself time to think that one sees what Bernard Shaw means. Human beings think they desire happiness, but its achievement would bore them to death: so how can it sensibly be said that this is what they desire? Another commonplace is that heaven would be boring: all those pious angels with their harps! For entertainment, one would have to go to hell. So again – what is meant by happiness? There is such confusion here that it is not surprising that human beings seem to get so little of what they say they want.

It seems to me that both sorts of truism are wrong – both that human beings desire happiness, and that if they got it it would be hell. I think these sorts of truism are maintained in order to protect a slothful *status quo*. What I think is true is that human beings do not particularly desire happiness but that it can be won by skill and hard work: and that if it were thus achieved, it would be a very pleasant state on earth.

What present-day human beings desire, it seems to me, is a condition in which they can be reassured as to their status and identity by a feeling of being superior to other people and by being able to complain: they like being one up on the people around them, and being resentful of anyone they think is trying to be one up on them. In this state people know just where they are: but it is a state not of happiness, but of power. It is also a condition of constant anxiety. A state of happiness is an absolution from anxiety; a feeling of being at one with other people and the universe; a conviction that in spite of the sorrows of the world, there is nothing of which to complain.

It is easy to pile up evidence that power is what people desire rather than happiness: for the most part nowadays in the Western world power takes the form of the possession of money. Most people would agree that large amounts of money do not bring happiness – there are popular songs and sayings to this effect – but few people surely would be eager to choose, if they had the magic choice, happiness rather than money. They might choose money and say that they believed that money would bring happiness: but to choose happiness knowing that it would not bring money – that would be a hard choice! Few people wish to become like present-day saints, however palpable their happiness.

Few psychoanalysts would suggest that human beings desire happiness. Freud described how people were torn between rival impulses towards sexuality and self-preservation: the peace that a person might hope to achieve was a precarious balance between the two. Jung described men as having to maintain themselves between competing archetypal forces that might destroy them: some sort of resolution might be achieved by skill, but the demand for skill was constant. In all this sort of understanding there is no suggestion that happiness is what people naturally desire: happiness is something constructed by intelligence and artistry out of the dangerous forces of impulses.

There are very few works of European literature – or indeed so far as I know of any literature – that are about happiness. What people like to read and to be reassured by are stories about characters even more tragic or sadly comic than they feel they are themselves. Lasting works of literature are for the most part to do with people who come to a sad end: and even when they seem to succeed – in getting married, for instance, at the very end of a book – there is usually the hint of how ephemeral this is, for soon their bubble of happiness will burst and they will be seen as silly as the older married couples that have been described around them. There is a sort of sub-literature of wish-fulfilment in which it is suggested that happiness might endure: but this is acceptable only if it is deliberately in the form of dreams. For representations of reality, what human beings require is that their own resentments and hurts should be reassured by the inabilities of others. This is what the ancient Greeks required from their tragedies, and it is what audiences require from the Theatre of the Absurd and the Theatre of Cruelty of the present day. Almost the only works of literature that might be said to be truly about happiness are to do not with human beings but with animals – *Winnie the Pooh* or *The Wind in the Willows*.

It seems to me that at the heart of all the preference for sadness is just the idea that human beings *should* desire happiness, and so when they do not, or when they do not get it, there is some guilt at the apparent failure but still some satisfaction in the guilt; because what an impossible idea it was anyway that human beings should desire happiness! There is even the idea that if the achievement of happiness is so obviously a dream, then there is nothing better for human beings to do than to give up all effort – and perhaps this is what human beings really want – for as Freud noted, another basic drive in human nature is the desire for release from tension and for death. So long as it is assumed that a state of happiness should be natural, then no start can be made on the hard graft towards achieving it. Skill and effort can only be applied when it is known that they are required.

In his play *Man and Superman*, from which the quotation at the beginning of this essay was taken, Bernard Shaw discourses about all this; especially in the long scene in the third act when Don Juan is in hell. Shaw demonstrates the propensity of human beings for hopelessness: but the argument, as so often in Shaw, is done with a view to charming the audience; to sending it away, however shocked, comfortably shocked – for what it will have been reassured by is that it is appreciative of cleverness and wit, just like the author. Perhaps Shaw had to keep everything he said as a bit of a joke; how else would he have got an audience to listen? But one of the themes of *Man and Superman* is just this – that human beings in their present state of evolution are not ready for anything so subtle and serious as happiness: what they

like to be reassured by are expressions of common despair and resentment – especially if these can be made out to be a bit of a joke. Shaw
suggested that before there could be any true embracing of happiness
a new type of human being would have to evolve – a type of man as
different from present man, in some respects, as present man is different
from the apes. Shaw used the word Superman deliberately in honour
of Nietzsche: but he does not elaborate much about Nietzsche in his
play. The way in which Nietzsche's idea of the Superman has come to
be misunderstood is that of the Superman being some sort of political
elitist (what a subject here for a Lying Truth!) whereas in fact Nietzsche
wrote in praise of someone who overcame not other people but himself.
The things that a man, in order to reach a higher state of evolution,
would have to overcome in himself, were just those things which, in
the present state of humanity, seem to be his ruling obsessions: the
desires for dominance, for resentment, for wary self-protection – what
Nietzsche called the Will to Power. The Will to Power was just what
the Superman would have to overcome in order to achieve happiness
– though Nietzsche did not exclusively use the word. But the question
remained: if the propensity of present-day human beings is towards
primitive attitudes such as dominance and resentment, how is it that
any effort towards the Superman can be encouraged?

   One reason perhaps why people find it so difficult to face the idea
that what human beings desire is not happiness is the thought that,
if this state of affairs is indeed true – if it is man's desire for power and
resentment that is innate – then there may be very little that he can
do about it, for no amount of effort can change his inborn character.
Once there seemed to be a God that might do this: if a person desired
change, and felt that change was not within his scope, then he could
pray to God to change him. After the so-called 'death of God' there
was a period in which it was thought that a man might pull himself up
by his own boots: but then there was Darwin, who seemed to suggest
that although a man might indeed change his environment, what was
innate in him he would not change: this could only change as a result
of a chance mutation and consequent natural selection. Thus a man,
so far as his basic propensities went, was at the mercy of chance: and
a chance that might bring about genetic change could be expected to
happen only once in countless years – and then most likely not to the
species' advantage. So what was there left for a man to do about his
lack of propensity for happiness other than to ignore it; or to pretend
it was something different by making jokes about it?

   Recently, however, there seems to have been a change in the views
held by some scientists – (scientists are apt to have a strong dislike,

may it be said in parenthesis, of sentences written by laymen beginning 'Recently, however, there seems to have been a change in the views held by some scientists . . .' Scientists are quick to claim that they are being misrepresented; that laymen do not understand their mysteries; that an attempt to translate their jargon into intelligible language is misconceived and dangerous. But these scientists, it seems to me, are exhibiting just those present-day propensities for resentment and will-to-power that should be challenged; and so) –

Recently, there seems to have been a change in the views held by some scientists: for although it is still held as true that innate genetic propensities cannot be directly affected by what has been learned, yet after all there may be some way of being able to talk as if characteristics acquired by effort might be passed on: for it seems there may be so many potential chance mutations already in existence within an organism – in existence as possibilities though latent and unexpressed – that some dispensation of circumstance might encourage some of these potentials to flourish which hitherto have not grown; and in this sense what might be passed on might be subject to human influence. A man's ability to control his circumstances, that is, might affect which innate result of chance is brought to the fore. So that if a few human beings wish to acquire a natural propensity for happiness, then there is in fact some point in their learning and practising happiness with skill and application; in the hope that in time this skill might become habitual; might even be passed on – that which previously had been innate but stifled becoming innate and expressed. Genetic propensities are like seeds; some may be dormant for a million years; but if there is a certain cultivation they might grow. But nothing new can grow – indeed there is little sense in the idea of cultivation – so long as it is assumed that men have no need of skills. The prerequisite for happiness is the realisation that happiness is not something easily desired: but it is something that can be created if its creation is desired.

Contribution to *Lying Truths*, a compilation edited by Ronald Duncan and Miranda Weston-Smith, 1979

'Two Cultures' Are No Culture

Contribution to the Science v. Humanities Debate

There is no sense in the idea of two concurrent cultures: a culture, if it is anything, is one. Certainly, there are two contemporary non-cultures, consisting of the bigots and the blinkered in either camp.

Bryan Appleyard, in his erudite and beautifully written book *Understanding the Present*, at times inveighs against science in the manner of a 1920s rationalist attacking Christianity: he takes as his target something called 'hard science' and condemns it for its cold materialistic inhumanity. In this way rationalists once used the attitudes of dogmatic fundamentalists to ridicule religion.

What is strange about Appleyard's book is that he then goes on to show that he is well aware that, in the further reaches of physics and biology, intelligent experts are now by no means materialistic, nor are they dismissive of the special status of humanity.

In quantum theory and chaos theory the view of a materialistic and determined world has been decisively undermined: there is now seen to be no rigid system of cause-and-effect; indeterminacy is established; things can validly be described as one thing or another (or both) according to the point of view. It is even suggested that the human ability to have a point of view is what determines what a thing shall be; the activity of an observer affects what is observed. A phrase was coined as early as the thirties: Reality is a function of the experimental condition. And it is humans who set the experimental conditions.

Thus to claim that science is distinct from what are called the 'humanities' on the ground that most workaday scientists do not ponder upon what their work implies, but for convenience go on treating both humans and the world as machines, is as superficial as the claim that a true representative of Christianity is the fundamentalist who takes the Bible to be literally 'true' (whatever that might mean) and has no regard for the staggering paradoxes of the story nor for the bizarre subtleties expressed, for instance, in the doctrine of the Trinity.

The claim made for the old-fashioned view of science is that it works: but so, in a sense, does simple fundamentalism – that is, it holds communities together and provides an impression of certainty. But both such claims are valid only at the cost of the refusal to use one's eyes and brain – so this indeed is a denial of humanity. The odd thing about Appleyard's book is that he seems to think it is just such a sense of certainty that humanity requires – though it is also just such a blindness in science that he rails against.

What makes Appleyard distrust and reject the observable complexities of modern science is that they are to do with uncertainty and change: and thus, he seems to think, they have no validity nor use for humans. But where on earth did he get the idea that there can be something in human life that provides a constant morality and a precisely definable meaning? There is nothing much of this in true religion. Christ did not say he was a set of definable precepts; he said he was the way, the truth and the life – to which people had to lay themselves open. Buddha taught that life – or a series of lives – was a movement, either to a lower level of the treadmill or to a blessed release. Tao, literally, means 'the way'. True religion has always been expressed in terms of a journey of discovery, a story, an unfolding of understanding.

Even those religionists who for the sake of easy communication try to codify their message usually recognise at some level that their efforts are shots at defining what is essentially indefinable; that their words are not truth but attempts at truth.

Similarly, most of the great physicists of the twentieth century – Bohr, Heisenberg, Schrodinger, Wheeler, Feynman – have acknowledged that both their equations and the images of the world formed from these are efforts at expressing reality or indeed at dealing with reality but they are not, except once more in some essentially indefinable sense, reality itself.

The evidence is that it is the purveyors of the two non-cultures that dogmatically insist on permanence and immutability; that a true culture acknowledges that each effort to understand reality is, in its own way, a process of learning; of a growing relationship with understanding. It does not matter – indeed it is inevitable – that one person's way is not the same as another's; what can be the same is the recognition of a quest and the demand for honesty and openness within it.

*

I had intended this piece to be on 'The Two Cultures and the Novel'; but it seemed this lengthy preamble was necessary for what I had to say.

Most novel writing nowadays is representative of the two non-cultures – of a vision of life in which humans are seen as automata or blinkered as to any chance of affecting their fate. Novelists are content to describe humans in terms of their helplessness or reactive oddities; not in terms of their powers of self-reflection and choice.

Even a novelist of such prodigious talent and powers of imagination as Iris Murdoch seems to weave her spells only to reach a point at which she can say that her miraculous constructions have been meaningless. In Murdoch's latest novel, *The Message to the Planet*, she seems for much of the time to be on the point of offering an eager reader just this – a weird and wonderful message, tantalisingly indefinable to be sure, but containing the sense that there is something vital to be glimpsed round some corner. But then, at the very end, she speaks loud and clear – 'Everything is accidental: that's the message.' But in this case how does one account for Murdoch's palpable creative genius; and indeed, people's appreciation of it?

This is an area in which the limitations that a philosopher sets herself surely have got the better of ordinary human experience. Everything seems accidental only if we surrender to the demands that nothing shall have meaning unless it can be pinned down in words. But as Bryan Appleyard points out, in spite of all our protestations about chance and determinism, we do in fact live as if we had choice and our lives had meaning; or at least we are apt to feel hard done by if they do not.

At the end of his book, Appleyard makes much of Wittgenstein's denial of the possibility of a private language. This argument runs: our thoughts and our understanding are dependent on language, but a language's meaning depends on its public use. But then Appleyard quotes Wittgenstein to the effect that the way our lives run has little to do with words: 'If I have exhausted the justification, I have reached bedrock and my spade is turned. Then I am inclined to say: "This is simply what I do." '

Novelists are in the unique position of being able to choose not only the words to describe what people do, but the attitudes that seem relevant to what they wish to effect. Novelists, that is, can suggest connections between human aspirations and what occurs.

Novelists are choosing, whether they like it or not, the sort of thing that they think life is or indeed could be – and it is just this, so scientists as well as poets tell us, that is within the creative power of humans. If, of course, novelists do not recognise that humans have any such power, then they are describing and indeed creating a world in which this is the case.

Bryan Appleyard in his book briefly mentions Nietzsche – he who announced the death of the idea of a God in relation to whom we were children, and demanded that we should grow up and take responsibility for the world, however terrible, upon ourselves.

Protagonists of the two non-cultures refuse to grow up; they continue to insist that the concept of responsibility has no meaning. But to those who wish to look and listen and learn, it seems indeed that there is a growing culture, although mysterious, through which we can begin to take responsibility on ourselves; and this culture has a comprehensiveness to describe which it might yet seem suitable to use a word such as God.

New Statesman, 1992

Part II
Literature and Reality

From *Journey into the Dark,* I

Some thirty years ago George Steiner asked a question that had been lurking in the darkness of people's minds and which still lies largely unanswered there – How is it that after some three thousand years of human culture, and especially the last two hundred since the Enlightenment, humans in the 1930s and '40s could perform, with apparent equanimity, such appalling and planned atrocities: how was it, specifically, that a man 'can read Goethe or Rilke in the evening, that he can play Bach and Schubert, and can go and do his day's work at Auschwitz in the morning?' (*Language and Silence*). Steiner dismissed as 'cant' the idea that people involved in such atrocities were uneducated or did not know what they were doing; also the idea that art, literature, have no bearing on human nature. 'To read Aeschylus or Shakespeare – let alone teach them – as if the texts, as if the authority of the texts in our own lives were immune from human history, is subtle but corrosive illiteracy'. Steiner insisted that the validity of Western culture, of the Western literary tradition, was being challenged by such a question. Fellow writers and critics for the most part ignored him – except to take exception to his view that there were necessary connections between literature and life.

A few years later Steiner returned to the question to try to give it his own answer. So far from the matter being incomprehensible, he suggested, if one stood back from the glare of accepted convention one might see how there might be quite straightforward connections between the Western literary tradition and twentieth-century horrors. He repeated his question – 'Why did humanistic traditions and models of conduct prove so fragile a barrier against political bestiality?' and then wondered – 'In fact were they a barrier, or is it more realistic to perceive in humanistic culture express solicitations of authoritarian rule and cruelty?' (*In Bluebeard's Castle*). Steiner argued that after the first enthusiasm for the Enlightenment, a paralysing reaction had set in: 'a marsh gas of boredom and vacuity thickened at various nerve-ends

of social and intellectual life'. Writers were soon crying out that bar-
barism was preferable to ennui; that such a propensity was intrinsic to
human nature. And thus – 'If we can come to understand the sources
of that perverse longing, of that itch for chaos, we will be nearer to an
understanding of our own state, and of the relations of our condition
to the accusing ideals of the past'. Much of the Romantic movement,
Steiner argued, was an expression of 'the nostalgia for disaster'; and a
representative post-Romantic work such as Flaubert's *Bouvard et Pécuchet*
was 'a long whine of loathing, of nausea at the apparently unshakeable
regime of middle-class values.' All such attitudes have been in effect
invitations to savagery – epitomised and not after all so frivolously in
the Dadaist proposition that an act of the highest virtue would be to
take a machine-gun and fire at random into a crowded street. How is it
then so surprising that Nazis, with their blinkered and pedantic minds,
would have wished to bring organisation to such proceedings?

Some thirty years after George Steiner's original agonised question,
a leading academic critic, Harold Bloom, has set out in *The Western
Canon* those books that he sees as generally accepted to be central to
the Western literary tradition. Bloom hardly disagrees with Steiner as
to the style of such works: he sees their common characteristic, that
which gives them potency, as what he calls *agon* – combat, antagonism,
strife. This has been the case since the time of the *Iliad*: 'What Homer
teaches is the poetics of conflict'. And the appeal of more demure
works has lain in the depiction of struggle concerning who will come
out on top: 'the aesthetic and the agonistic are one'. Also this has
been the style by which one work rather than another has found its
way into the canon and has stayed there: a work has 'to win the agon
with tradition'. Literature, that is, is formed and survives by a contest
to see which work will prove fittest; and the mark of fitness is just the
effective description of such internecine struggles.

Where Bloom differs from Steiner is in his contention that this style
and such attitudes in literature have little effect on human behaviour:
'Reading the very best writers – let us say Homer, Dante, Shakespeare,
Tolstoy – is not going to make us better citizens': but neither is it going
to make us worse citizens, for – 'art is perfectly useless, according to
the sublime Oscar Wilde who is always right'. Bloom even goes into
counter-attack against writers who 'believe that literary criticism could
become a basis for democratic education or societal improvement. . . .
Scholars who urge us to find the source of our morality and our politics
in Plato, or in Isaiah, are out of touch with the social reality in which we
live. If we read the Western canon in order to form our social, political
or personal or moral values, I firmly believe we will become monsters

of selfishness and exploitation'. By this Bloom seems to be referring to the tendency of politically orientated groups to expropriate works of literature for their own propagandist ends. But then has not such battle for expropriation and exploitation, in his view, constituted much of the substance and style of the Western canon? It is the spectre perhaps of such inconsistency that has led Bloom to take his stand against the idea of connections between literature and life: he loves the stories of selfishness and savagery in the Western canon; he does not wish to seem to love selfishness and savagery in life. But as Steiner has remonstrated – what is the worth of a literature that has nothing to do with life?

Bloom in fact does eventually suggest criteria other than the effective depiction of struggle by which works find their place within the canon: qualities that are further required are those of 'strangeness' and 'originality'. But such qualities in his view are still to be seen only with reference to other works within the canon; no need is recognised for an original view of life. But then as if still haunted by the spectre of this hermetic view of literature, Bloom does propose for it some personal efficacy: literature may after all, he says, be that which 'enables us to learn how to talk to ourselves and endure ourselves. . . . All that the Western canon can bring one is the proper use of one's own solitude, that solitude whose final form is one's confrontation with one's own mortality'. Such an enablement might indeed seem to be useful – though still with respect to a relationship with death. About life, in this view of literature, there remains little to be learned. But should this not be seen as what was designated some seventy years ago as a *trahison des clercs* – a treacherous abandonment by intellectuals of any heartfelt struggle with life?

George Steiner saw the dangers for literary criticism and indeed for literature if what was at stake was no more than the outcome of contest, of game-playing – even if the style of this was practice for a confrontation with death. 'Literary criticism becomes no longer a very interesting or responsible exercise. . . . Books about books, and that flourishing though still recent genre, books about literary criticism (a threefold remove) will no doubt continue to pour out in great numbers. But it is becoming clear that most of them are a kind of initiate sport, that they have little to say to those who would ask what coexistence and interaction are possible between humanism, between the idea of literate communication, and the present shape of history'. Literary criticism becomes a display like basketball, in which lumbering players leap and cavort and score points with skill, but this has little relevance to anything but the game. And when a passionate critic such as Steiner runs on to the field of play then he appears like some anarchist or streaker, and there is nothing for players to do but wait for him to be removed so that they can get on with the game.

The reason usually given for why humans not only enjoy watching or reading about the mocked-up antics of, say, tormented Greek kings and murderous Scottish landowners but even claim to find them uplifting is, of course, the poetry – those melodious tones and rhythms that seem to thrive on depictions of mayhem and despair but yet by the nature of their beauty to suggest the possibility of something different – something that might be occurring after all off-stage. Aristotle suggested that by observing rituals of savagery and hatred on a stage an audience might be purged of such tendencies within themselves. But as both Steiner and Bloom point out – Steiner with alarm, Bloom with equanimity – this does not seem to be what occurs. Tragedies may indeed offer guide-lines on the way to death, but there is still no evidence of encouragement for life. Bloom continues to try to find an escape from the trap of uselessness he has set for himself: 'Iago and Edmund and Hamlet contemplate themselves objectively in images wrought by their own intelligences and are enabled to see themselves as dramatic characters, aesthetic artifices. They thus become free artists of themselves, which means that they are free to write themselves, to will changes in the self. Overhearing their own speeches and pondering those expressions, they change and go on to contemplate an otherness in the self, or the possibility of such otherness'. But for all the self-contemplation of Iago and Edmund and Hamlet they are characters who in fact do not manage to change: they remain trapped within the contexts of their obsessions with vengeance and death. But then – if they had indeed been able to demonstrate some possible otherness in the self, would they not have upset the accepted conventions of the stage; might they not have seemed like freedom-fighters or streakers disrupting the field of play?

The Shakespearean performances that have given the most lively excitement to myself at least have in fact been those rare ones in which the actors have seemed to behave in something of this way: in overhearing their own speeches and pondering their expressions they have seemed to give intimations of some real 'otherness in the self' – and one concerned with life beyond the death-obsessed confines of the stage. It is as if these actors were saying – What on earth am I doing trapped within this character and with these obsessions; are not these just conventions for an actor on a stage? Alec Guinness's *Hamlet* in the 1950s for instance – reviled by most critics but passionately admired by a few – was a performance in which the actor seemed to be aware of himself embodied in a role in front of an audience; to be attentive to this predicament; to be glancing towards the audience from time to time as if saying – Look, we all know we are in some way confronted by, or constrained within, such ghastly characters or circumstances as this; why else except in respect of such recognition do we go to a play? but insofar as we can know this, and can let others know that we know this, can we not also – in life as on a stage – get off-stage; get out? We accept that Hamlet has to die: can we not also remember that we, audience and actor, can go home?

This was the acting style that the playwright Brecht advocated – so that his plays should seem not just as fabrications but as representative of life.

Even an iconoclast such as George Steiner however seems to have felt the weight, the near inevitability, of characters and actors and audience being trapped within a game; of the outrage that would be caused by anyone subverting the rules of play. He remarks (in *After Babel*) on the 'nausea' that would overcome an audience if, for instance, Agamemnon in the *Oresteia* suddenly decided to hop aside and avoid his fate; if Oedipus simply gave up the lacerating enquiry into his father's death. But for a few exhausted watchers who have seen it all before – might there not be some relief? Might there not be pleasure, that is, in a recognition on the stage of the sort of idea that must, goodness knows, occasionally flit through some minds in an audience – We will before long be able to slip away from this uproar: might there be a chance of bumping into those who have acted Oedipus or Ophelia at the Café Royal?

Both George Steiner and Harold Bloom see in any assessment of literature the central importance of Shakespeare – George Steiner with some distrust, Harold Bloom placing him alone at the summit of the Western canon. Steiner agrees with Wittgenstein that there is something in Shakespeare that is not quite 'true to life': actors love acting him because 'his brushstrokes are so individual that each one of his characters looks significant'. But he is the supreme *wordsmith* rather than prophet or teacher; the ingredient which he lacks is the 'ethical, salvational function' of the true *Dichter* or truth-saying poet (*No Passion Spent*). To Bloom, with his insistence that literature has little relevance to life, this would hardly be a failing. But what neither Steiner nor Bloom give attention to in their assessments of Shakespeare are his late so-called 'miracle' plays – *The Winter's Tale*, *Cymbeline*, *Pericles* – which precisely are concerned with an 'ethical, salvational function'. So what is it about these plays that makes it possible for them to be ignored even by those most concerned to lament the absence of, or deny the relevance of, such a function? The point seems to be that whatever is ethical and salvational about them – that by which wrong-doings and misfortunes may be worked through and redeemed – does not seem directly to do with the dramatics and declamations occurring on stage; it seems rather to be effected precisely by what may be gathered to be going on off-stage – with the bizarre patterns of coincidence and connection and renewal that are for the most part unseen but which float into view as if on some cosmic tide or curve. These may then leave seeds which can take root if the ground has been prepared; and with effects that can seem like miracles. But in fact are there not in the normal course of events in life strange patterns of coincidence and conjunction which can take root as it were if they are recognised? What seems to be unnatural in these plays to some observers is that salvation seems not only unmerited but unlikely: there may be sorrow and repentance, but redemption seems to come from beyond the bounds of cause and effect. But then again – do not such occasions and coincidences seem representative of those rare chances from which life springs, and which are in contrast to what seems inevitable about death? In *Cymbeline* it is true that the off-stage/on-stage machinations often seem absurd; in *The Winter's Tale* they are somewhat abrupt. But in *Pericles* – much of which is deliberately in the form of a masque and thus in recognition of the style and limitations of a stage – the long recognition scene between Pericles and Marina is one in which there do seem dazzlingly to be connections with forces from outside: characters and audience weep not only for the events but for what is felt as a visitation of grace. If in most of his work Shakespeare saw all the world as a stage, in his last years he seemed to know that which is beyond it.

For what is being recognised here – and what is the concern of all those whom Steiner and Wittgenstein refer to as prophets and truth-saying poets – is that if there is to be any vision of life beyond histrionics and game-playing, then it is not enough to contemplate oneself or one's behaviour as an aesthetic artefact; not enough to ruminate on the difficulties or chances of becoming something other; what is necessary is to recognise or at least to be alert to what in fact might be going on unseen. For this one has to watch, to listen, not to imagine that one necessarily knows. One has to be conscious of possibilities, which by their nature are for the most part in the dark. To be able to do this there has to be some trust – that there exists in the darkness that which might be responsive to one's trust. But in a world of possibilities there can at least be the chance to see if this is so. In Shakespeare's late plays there is not only the poetry that gives intimations of an unseen order but also the patterning of events by which order seems able to be found within mundane chaos – by any-one, perhaps, who has learned to be attentive to such a possibility. Such an experience is the opposite of anything to do with *agon* – though the process of learning is likely to have arisen and been endured not without struggle and even fear. Such learning is a recognition both of the self and of that otherness in the self that it has learned to recognise; which has been both merited and not merited as is the case with any grace. Attentiveness becomes the condition by which so-called miracles may be seen as natural; these coincidences being in the order of things like beauty or poetry.

George Steiner in *Real Presences* proposed that the very fact that art, literature, exist, is evidence for a mode of being beyond that of appearances; what else is it that art, poetry, give intimations of? They offer glimpses of whatever is behind the scenes. This whatever-it-is is unlikely to be able to be clearly put into words (why else should there be the need for art, for poetry?). Such invitations to glimpse can be accepted or refused; but the chance of knowing is there. This experi-ence leads not so much to illumination as to an awareness of presence in the dark. Steiner writes – 'I will put forward the argument that the experience of aesthetic meaning in particular, that of literature, of the arts, of musical form, infers the necessary possibility of this "real presence". The seeming paradox of "necessary possibility" is, very precisely, that which the poem, the painting, the musical composition are at liberty to explore and to enact'. Such understanding can be approached, known, attended to: it can scarcely be defined: and the turning towards it remains a matter of choice. Steiner accepts that the word 'God' once referred to that which was thus experienced – to the confidence that, if whatever occurred or were to occur were trusted, this could be experienced as acceptable. This was akin to the experi-ence of an artist who seems to uncover rather than to create what is there: it is also that which the true artist tries to express – which is the way the world unfolds itself. The words become tentative: use of the word 'God' is always a matter of choice. But whatever words are risked, if they are too much dissected and analysed, then whatever has been found is likely to die in the light.

That such intimations of otherness linger on even in this glittering fragmented Western world is not, Steiner argues, because we are still frightened of old ghosts, but because there are so many experiences vital to people's daily lives that can only be looked at and responded to by such recognitions. Even in old religious dispensations there were warnings that a word such as 'God' should not be vainly used: but 'necessary possibilities' – 'real presences' – such vagueness perhaps gives due deference to the dark. People have to go on their own journeys – for the sake of themselves, for the sake of their non-selves, to discover what these might be; for the sake of (but say no more!) that which they will find. With recognition there may come enlightenment; but it will be from the sort of light that is in fact everywhere, and which until it comes up against an object seems to be dark.

The question which George Steiner posed and which was quoted at the beginning of this essay has no answer if it is looked for within the limits of light. It can seem rational to argue that literature had no connection with life; it is not absurd to argue that the style of Western literature has been such that what is surprising is not that there have been so many atrocities in history but that there have not been more. The philosopher Adorno suggested that after Auschwitz there could be no more poetry: and if by this is meant there should be no more ennoblement of horror by the glorious use of words, then he is surely right. For our daily entertainment it still seems to be our nature to enjoy shadowy spectacles of murder and torture, dismemberment and disgust: these seem to give us strange reassurance. But for meaning – for trying to understand or deal with or even possibly change our so evident propensity for horror – we have to go on a journey into the dark.

Unpublished, 1998

What Are Novels For?

In the 1940s when I was young it seemed that anyone interested in literature was aware of what was called 'the great tradition' of English novel writing. I had not then read F. R. Leavis, but I took it for granted that a mainstream ran through Jane Austen, George Eliot, Henry James, D. H. Lawrence. These writers and their characters were concerned with 'moral preoccupations'; such preoccupations were the result of 'a vital capacity for experience, a kind of reverent openness before life'(Leavis). These novelists and their characters wanted to find out how life worked – what were the connections, if any, between the inner attitude and the outer event; were humans helpless, or had they some small influence over their fate? There was another stream of novel writing, which became known as 'modernist', that swirled and eddied around James Joyce and Virginia Woolf: the preoccupations of these writers were not so much moral as observational and descriptive; they were concerned with developing a style which would illuminate what went on in the mind and in the outside world but there was little differentiation and thus little to-and-fro between the two, and thus not much of an area in which moral activity might have meaning.

When I was a would-be novelist my early love was William Faulkner – who seemed to combine a prodigiously inventive style with a concern for how life worked. His characters seldom triumphed, but they learned to survive; or if they did not, they accepted what they had brought on themselves. At the back of Faulkner's novels – as with those of Henry James, who was the novelist I most revered in the 'great tradition' – was the sense that life was such that if you adopted certain attitudes, behaved in a certain way, then certain consequences were likely to follow. You could not tell with any accuracy what these might be, but you could learn to have an inkling of their nature – and to trust that the world was such that such probabilities existed. It was in this sense that here were the preoccupations that could be called moral. It was this that provided the tensions and the dramatic interest of the stories.

It is this sense that has become largely lost among literary novels in the West. What has prevailed is the fashion of seeing life as a matter of one thing happening after another; of depicting humans as having little or no chance of ordering their fate. It is in this style that readers seem able to feel at home. Their interest is helped by the practice of portraying characters that are bizarre, and events that are considered to be outlandish or taboo.

In the 'great tradition' of English novel writing moral preoccupations were worked out in relation to society; something was learned by characters and offered to readers with reference to the mechanisms of a social structure that they accepted. Jane Austen's Emma, for instance, learns to look at and to repent of her snobbish insensitivity within a social framework which gives 'learning' and 'insensitivity' meaning. The happy ends of Jane Austen's novels depend on the social convention that a marriage is a happy event – though, in fact, there is little in her novels to suggest that life after marriage is happy. But the convention was strong enough to make the optimism seem valid.

In the great novels of Henry James's middle period – *What Maisie Knew*, and *The Awkward Age* – the young protagonists learn what they do of human nature in relation to the machinations of the corrupt society around them; however much they are seen as superior to this society, there is no escape from it. In D. H. Lawrence's novels, the heroes and heroines plunge into strange locations of body and mind in their efforts to re-form moribund social patterns; but they too do not see themselves morally operative apart from some form of society.

It is this idea that morality or meaning is found and worked out in relation to society that seems to have broken down. In this Freudian, Nietzschean and now post-Marxist age, it is seen that concepts of morality are all too often mechanisms by which certain sections of society struggle to maintain their dominance over others. And even personal morality – sanctified by obeisance to a God or to a humanist concept such as the greatest happiness of the greatest number – can be seen as a manipulation to maintain one's sense of superiority and safety. The pursuit of social or political morality has often, to be sure, led societies and individuals into self-destructive as well as destructive paths; but then it can be suggested that this also is a predilection of humans – to find satisfaction in forms of immolation.

It is this sort of realisation that has rendered unfashionable novels to do with moral preoccupations. If the sense of the virtue of con-ventional society has broken down, how can morality and meaning be sought in relation to it? And since also the belief in a relationship with a transcendent God has largely broken down – together with the belief in any sort of absolute definable by man – indeed, it might be asked what is left for a writer to write about, except the confrontation with a mad and meaningless world in which humans can do no better than hang on by their fingertips. This is the train of events that has seemed unavoidable: old forms of life, or of belief, do inevitably change and die – even if this is a prerequisite of the chance for new ones to grow. And so, perhaps, for a time novels have had to be about humans as almost mindless creatures obsessed with sex and violence and shopping; about whom and for whom stories can be written as diversions for an idle moment.

But there is something in the writing of even such novels – in the writing even of the critics who praise such novels – that belies the sort of situation that is being depicted. For, in fact, all storytelling, all criticism even, is a way of bringing order out of chaos: so that there is something self-contradictory and indeed somewhat blind about stories and criticism that present humans as helpless and absurd. And this, it seems to me, is the situation which, by this time, could be recognised and avoided. For there are other areas of inquiry and activity that suggest possibilities of moral preoccupations having meaning: it is just difficult, at the moment, to find a suitable language in which to talk about such things.

There are scientists, for instance, who are making discoveries about the propensity of matter, of energy, to create order out of chaos; of the potentiality of humans to affect patterns behind the cause-and-effect mechanisms of everyday events. Such scientists are David Bohm in physics, Ilyia Prigogine in chemistry, Rupert Sheldrake in biology. They naturally have difficulty in putting the strikingly original results of their observations into traditionally acceptable words – whether conventional or scientific. One corollary of their mode of understanding, indeed, is that a person has to make a creative effort to get in the way of it on his own: that what is being discovered is perhaps just what is meant by understanding. But the point that emerges is that this effort is possible – human consciousness and the outside world are such that the recognition and indeed the formation of patterns of connection and interaction are possible – however much these processes go on partly in the dark, and the language to describe them has to be to some extent metaphorical.

There is also an enormous amount of work being done in psychology and psychotherapy in which understanding is being formulated about the ways in which humans are (and are not) responsible for their fate; ways in which others can (and cannot) help them. People can look at the facts of their case; can be encouraged to do this by others; and by these means healing and change may take place – but no one can force this process. Here too, the results of experience are difficult to pin down in words: a too precise delineation can counteract the learning that is being encouraged. It has to be accepted that words are often no more than shots at describing unique requirements; not prescriptions for laying down general rules. There has been much mystification in this area as a result of the jargon used by so-called New Age thinkers – and there is much justified criticism of this. But it is the curse nowadays even of such critics that, if they wish to have anything positive to say, are apt to find themselves resorting to jargon.

It has seemed to me that there is a valid role for novels here – to portray the networks of influences and patterns which can be glimpsed behind the facades of everyday events; which, in fact, are glimpsed instinctively, however difficult it is to describe these didactically. Such patterns are often paradoxical – to do with the way in which good can sometimes come out of evil (though this does not imply that evil can be advocated); the way in which inner decision can affect the outer event (though this latter may well not be what one has intended). These are matters not of certainty but of impression; but then it has always been the function of poems and stories to evoke resonances and meanings that can be presented in no better way. So what is it nowadays, even after the crack-up of conventional religion and society, that stops this sort of thing becoming fashionable in novels?

Perhaps there is some burden put on readers when faced with this sort of inquiry. It is as if they are being told – Look, you are not helpless; there are things to be learned; there are attitudes to be adopted or discarded. There may be no more guide-lines given by society or by God; and to be sure, you are not expected to join some New Age group; but however much in the dark, there are patterns in life to be found on your own. The nature of these can be presented to you in the form of stories; but then you may be free to feel, or have to deny, that they are relevant to your own life story.

But if you are a Professor of Literature or a professional critic, what on earth are you to make of this? How can there be academic discipline if what is being said is – Watch, listen; and learn to go your own ways? In fact, certain academic so-called disciplines have emerged in recognition of the force of such ideas. The schools of structuralism and deconstruction arose as a result of the breakdown of social and literary conventions; these schools deny that a literary text refers to any reality apart from that of the interpretation of a critic or reader. But it is at this point that such academic critics find themselves resorting, because they are still denying there is any meaning to 'meaning', to a hideous jargon that makes the mumbo-jumbo of occultists seem lucid. It seems that there has to be some sort of academic gravy-train to keep the literary show going: poets and novelists, after all, are apt to back away from, or slip under, the wheels of trains. But what of the dedicated few who sit in fields, as it were, with their backs to the rails?

The sort of novelists and novels I am referring to when I talk about individuals finding their way through the maze of an apparently disintegrating social world – following the promptings of what seems to be an integrating larger whole – such novels have been, for instance, in comparatively recent years, J. D. Salinger's *Franny and Zooey*, Saul Bellow's *Mr. Sammler's Planet*, *The Eighth Day* by Thornton Wilder. In the first, the young girl Franny, having been driven to clinical depression by the insanity of the social world around her, is rescued from this by her younger brother Zooey by means of a controlled effort of creative imagination. This story was ridiculed by critics, and Salinger stopped publishing his works. In the second, Mr Sammler stalks through the manifestations of a sick society with the authoritative and admonitory eye of an Old Testament prophet. But critics have preferred other books by Saul Bellow in which heroism is more anarchic. And in the third – but how many people now read *The Eighth Day*, in which the operations of sanctity, of the Spirit, are worked out with mysterious but almost didactic precision? Of course, this can be called mumbo-jumbo. Among recent English novelists, I can think easily of only John Fowles as someone who has dealt memorably and in an original way with moral preoccupations.

I have suggested there is a burden passed on in such novels, but it should be the burden of liberation. Wittgenstein suggested that there are things about which, if one is to respect the bounds of conventional language, one should keep silent. The novels I have been talking about do presuppose the existence of some transcendent force of order – of the activity of what, for want of a better word, one might call grace. And about God there has always been a well-documented case for keeping silent. But then, God has also always properly been talked about in stories. And does not the fact that there are stories imply the ability of humans to procreate?

Times Literary Supplement, 1992

William Faulkner's Universe

In his Nobel Prize acceptance speech in 1949 William Faulkner said –

> The young man or woman writing today has forgotten the problems of the
> human heart in conflict with itself, which alone can make good writing
> because only that is worth writing about, worth the agony and the sweat.
> He must learn them again, he must teach himself that the basis of all things
> is to be afraid, and teaching himself that, forget it for ever, leaving no room
> in his workshop for anything but the old verities and truths of the heart
> – the old universal truths lacking which any story is ephemeral and doomed
> – love and honour and pity and pride and compassion and sacrifice.

In England Faulkner is still not widely read, and even appreciative critics mainly think of him as the inventor of something called
the Deep South, or complain of the complexity of his style. There is
little discussion of his work in such terms as he describes in his Nobel Prize speech. This may be due to an English tradition by which
a writer does not trust words like compassion and sacrifice. But the
speech quoted above continues – 'Until he does so he labours under
a curse, he writes not of love but of lust, of defeats in which nobody
loses anything of value, of victories without hope . . .' Whatever the
cause, Faulkner himself believes that in the literary arena there are
two sets of protagonists – of one of which he would be the passionate
champion.

From the first he has been a novelist who writes not only about
sequences of events but about how people experience them, influence
them, understand them. His complex style is an attempt to express this:
he has gone beyond straight narrative description into a mingling, or
juxtaposition, of things that are happening, people's thoughts about
these happenings, and people's talking about them. There is also this
complexity, or writing in several dimensions, in the structure of each
book: different parts of the book, sometimes describing slightly differently the same events, are told through the eyes of different characters.

All this is held together by the overwhelming flow of his words and sentences, which rises at times to great heights of wit and beauty. And by these techniques he does achieve an extraordinary sense of the mystery and complexity of life as it is experienced, in contrast to a narrative style which remains outside.

He achieves, also, a sense of the 'verities' which he says are the only things worth writing about. If you want to describe honour and sacrifice you have to assume free will: if you want to assume this you have to have a dimensional space (in writing as in life as it were) to move within. The writers of a straight narrative style are often those who seem implicitly to deny free will. Faulkner's very technique is part of his beliefs about man and literature.

His earliest books – *Soldier's Pay, Mosquitoes* – demonstrate this. (*Mosquitoes* is also one of the funniest books ever written.) The most technically extreme was *The Sound and the Fury* published in 1929. In this, the first seventy pages are told through the mind of an idiot who cannot distinguish between the present and memory; the next hundred are told by a character who died twenty years previously; and the third and fourth parts happen twenty years later again. The effect of this is unique, I believe, in literature: after a fascinated reading for hours with only a chaotic idea of what is going on, there dawns on one, in an intensely exciting flash around page 250, not only exactly what is happening there, on page 250, but the whole meaning and actual events of all the book in one moment. This is the equivalent of scales falling from confused eyes in life.

Also in these books there began to appear the Faulkner characters who are not only individuals but are seen as archetypes, thus adding yet another dimension to Faulkner's 'reality' – the two young girls, the one vacant and sensuous and the other intent and virginal (Jenny and Patricia of *Mosquitoes*); the wild and celibate young man who tries to do good (Joe of *Soldier's Pay* and the reporter of *Pylon*); the predatory hordes like Wagner's dwarfs who sell their souls for money. *Pylon* is the book with which to begin Faulkner: the dramatic background is that of a 1920s air-circus. A good second book would be *The Wild Palms*, a romantic tragedy – the only time Faulkner lets his celibate man and passionate woman go off with each other. *Light in August* is the largest scaled, most beautifully written, and probably the best book to stand on its own.

But also during this his first period (the period between the two wars) another whole string of books began to appear, books that were published separately but which seemed to be a part of, or aspects of, a much larger whole – a place, a population, a history of a hundred

years. The place was Yoknapatawpha County in the state of Missis-
sippi: the books *Sartoris, As I Lay Dying, Absalom, Absalom!* There
were also short stories about characters that had been mentioned in
other stories, about events that had previously been treated but not
so exhaustively. Then in 1940 came *The Hamlet,* a sort of watershed
in Faulkner's development, a large novel that contained not only
two of his most astonishing prose set-pieces (the description of Eula
Varner, the story of the wild ponies) but also in clear outline now the
histories of the Snopes family and the Varner family and the country
around Jefferson, thus tying up loose ends and being a source of endless ramifications for the future.

　　After *The Hamlet* there were more short stories, short novels, going
backwards and forwards in time, many of them centering on the lawyer
Gavin Stevens – the last and most evolved of Faulkner's celibates.
There was *A Fable,* the most obscure and powerful of Faulkner's later
self-contained works. Then in 1957 there was *The Town,* another long
novel and a direct continuation of *The Hamlet:* and now published
in England, *The Mansion* – the last book of the trilogy and which,
Faulkner says, is 'the final chapter of, and the summation of, a work
conceived and begun in 1925'.

　　It is almost impossible to overrate this achievement. What Faulkner
has done, and what it becomes apparent he has uniquely succeeded in
doing, is to have extended the purpose and comprehensiveness of his
style from the limits of individual books into what he calls a 'living
literature'. It is now not only the parts of each book that illuminate and
give meaning to the whole, but each book that expands and slightly
alters everything before and after. This is not only an extraordinary
aesthetic achievement: it is, again, like life itself – at least if you share
Faulkner's beliefs about free will and eternal verities. For by creating a
place and a history as well as a style he has given himself a framework
in which not only freedom but providence have meaning. In searching
for a parallel, one is reminded of Wagner, but he did not have the wit;
or of Proust, but he did not have the social scope. By the unflagging
inventiveness and the magic with words one is reminded (and of
whom else dare one say this?) of Shakespeare.

　　There are occasional small doldrums in the trilogy – mainly in
the details of the Snopeses' financial swindles, with which, perhaps
unluckily, the first two books start. But *The Mansion* is almost all a
triumph; though it is difficult to imagine what a reader would make
of it who knew nothing else of the history. The gnome-like Snopeses
destroy one another by their internecine betrayals (as a character in
The Town says – 'they none of them seemed to bear any specific kin-

ship to one another; they were just Snopeses, like rats and termites are just rats and termites'). The approach to the murder at the end of *The Mansion* has the nightmarish and doomed intensity of the best of *Light in August*.

But also starting with the second book of the trilogy there have been the other and opposed characters – those who have some sort of freedom within the turmoil of the others' machinations. These are treated more fully here than anywhere else in Faulkner – the archetypal two women and the man being brought to consummation in Eula ('as muscleless and fluid as a miraculous intact milk'), Linda ('tall like a heron out of a moil of frogs and tadpoles'), and Gavin ('smug and inscrutable and arrogant and immune as a louse on a queen's arse'). The relationships and struggles for probity and influence between these characters come to a climax in the love between Gavin and Linda, who want to possess one another but who (Linda is deaf, so that while she talks Gavin has to write down comments on a piece of paper, thus adding another technical dimension to Faulkner's uncanny creation) 'are the two in all the world who can possess each other without having to'.

All Faulkner's work is in a sense tragic because it deals with the price paid for the experiences of love and freedom. But it is also profoundly hopeful. One of his greatest achievements here is to have reaffirmed superbly his own faith and what he says should be the faith of all writers – and which he repeats (he is never afraid of repetition) at the end of his Nobel Prize speech –

> I believe that man will not merely endure, he will prevail – he is immortal not because he alone among creatures has an inexhaustible voice, but because he has a soul, a spirit capable of compassion and sacrifice and endurance. The poet's, the writer's duty is to write about these things. . . . The poet's voice need not merely be the record of man, it can be one of the props, the pillars, to help him endure and prevail.

Time and Tide, 1961

Seeing It Whole

The Twyborn Affair. By Patrick White

In Patrick White's novels human beings are seen within a landscape. They do not dominate; they are part of a whole which sometimes gives them dignity and sometimes bemuses them, but which never makes them meaningless. They are often at the mercy of forces inside them; but these, too, seem representative of forces within the whole, so that it is as if human beings are able to be in some working relationship with this whole, even though they do not control it.

In *The Twyborn Affair,* the forces inside the partly mythical hero/heroine are those of bisexuality. Eddie/Eadith Twyborn is seen first as a girl living with a much older man in the South of France just before the First World War. The revelation that he/she is, in fact, a boy is a literary tour de force: the reader has for some time felt there is something wrong about the relationship; then it is realised that this is exactly what the writer has intended. In this first part of the book, the mysterious presentation wonderfully parallels the ambiguities of what is described.

In the second part, Eddie/Eadith reappears as Lt Twyborn DSO, on a ship going home to Australia after the war. There he works on a sheep farm; he tries to establish his masculine identity. Both the foreman on the farm and the wife of the owner fall in love with him, and he lets himself be seduced; what is androgynous in him is also magical. But such magic, in the society in which he lives, is destructive. A person can only fit into this society by pretending to push the bisexuality that is in himself or herself, and which is in everybody, to one extreme or the other. This pretence is achieved by most of the minor characters in the book, but only at disastrous cost to themselves and to society.

In the final part of the book Eddie/Eadith reappears as the 'madam' of a London brothel just before the Second World War. She provides sex for members of the English upper class. In this role of procuress he/she seems to have found the right ecological niche. She is the provider of women for the gratification of men; she has come to terms with her bisexual predicament by treating it as a business. But after a time her own feelings break in; as does war, again, to break up a cankerous society.

Patrick White's novels have always moved between, or embraced, the levels of realism and myth. It is his excellence as a writer on both levels that gives him his power; also, perhaps, his tendency to make critics uneasy. Critics, on the whole, seem to like realism as realism and myth as myth: the marriage of the two is indeed somewhat magical. But to those who believe, as I do, that what is 'real' is seen always through the eyes of some mental mythology, and that to be able to appreciate such mythology is necessary to recognise what is real – to such people, Patrick White's novels are on a higher level of interest than those of almost any other novelist writing today.

The first and third parts of the book take place just before a world war in which humans tear each other to pieces. The mythology here is one in which the tearing-apart of the outside world is symptomatic of the bisexual split within persons (also perhaps of the split in seeming to be part animal and part god). War is the expression of people who push parts of themselves towards poles; they seem unable to love themselves as complexities of masculine and feminine. Eddie/Eadith does at least accept herself; and so she accepts her neighbours. Most of the other characters in the book, particularly Eddie/Eadith's parents, hate and fear parts of themselves and so hate and fear their neighbours.

The realism of the first two parts of the book is marvellously exact: Patrick White seems as much at home on the Riviera of 1914 as he is in the Australian outback of 1920. The part of the book that seems at first sight most foreign is that to do with London of the 1930s: how reptilian are these denizens of Chelsea! (The author uses the word 'squamous'). But then, it seems, might not Patrick White, an Australian, see something about the English that we do not easily see ourselves? There is a country house-party which is reminiscent of those in *Brideshead Revisited:* but how much more sinister and less charming! Perhaps it is part of English people's false mythology to see themselves as charming – as indeed readers were warned in *Brideshead Revisited.*

In his other books, notably *Riders in the Chariot* and *The Vivisector,* Patrick White has suggested ways in which people might have chances of avoiding the extremes of brandished toughness or assumed tenderness which are at the poles of their bisexuality – or indeed of learning something better than the skills of business-like manipulation. In these two books the ways suggested are those of a saint and an artist. In *The Twyborn Affair*, Eddie/Eadith is neither; but he/she does see her predicament and faces it with courage, and in the social context this seems to be a significant achievement.

It is sometimes said of Patrick White's novels that his protagonists do not quite seem creatures of flesh and blood. But flesh and blood are not, in the context of the larger landscape, the most interesting parts of a person; they are usually to do with histrionics. The more interesting parts are to do with consciousness, elegance, wisdom. It is of these that Patrick White writes: also of colours, shapes, sights, smells – apart from histrionics. He has evolved a wonderfully witty and allusive style to deal with all this; one which can describe both unfortunate things and transcendental things with empathy and de-tachment. He has one foot in the earth and the other heaven knows where – which is a good position for any colossus.

Listener, 1979

What Life Is Like

If on a winter's night a traveller. By Italo Calvino

From time to time speculative writers are struck by the idea that straightforward story-telling imposes a simplicity on experience that reality does not have: people enjoy a good story just because it possesses a form which they can hope or imagine, even if in vain, might be representative of life. In fact human life is a matter of multifarious interlocking dramas, false starts, unfinished strands, might-have-beens, which jostle for the attention of consciousness; and however enjoyable for a time it might be to suppose otherwise, such a pretence involves falsification and thus in the end a disappointment with reality.

Italo Calvino has been a writer of original and beautifully detailed fantasies – notably *The Nonexistent Knight* and *The Baron in the Trees*. In these he employed a fantasy form deliberately to describe the predicaments of people somewhat desperately trying to conform to, or refusing to conform to, conventions about life. Now, in *If on a winter's night a traveller,* he moves on to the ground of demonstrating the difficulties of writing a book that is neither a fantasy nor to do with conventions but is, on the other hand, however confusingly, aiming at being both accurate and hopeful about life. The form of his interweaving stories leading on, from and into one another is similar to that of *The Thousand and One Nights* or Goethe's *Wilhelm Meister:* but there is the added dimension here that the writer is explaining to the reader what he is doing, and is anxious that the reader shall share some of the responsibility.

The book opens with the words: 'You are about to begin reading Italo Calvino's new novel'. Two-thirds of the way through there is the remark: 'I have had the idea of writing a novel composed only of the beginnings of novels. The protagonist could be a reader who is continually interrupted. The Reader buys the new novel A by the author Z. But it is a defective copy, he can't go beyond the beginning.

59

He returns to the bookshop to have the volume exchanged'.

And, in the meantime, this is just the novel that Italo Calvino has been writing. The Reader's book seems to have been wrongly bound; in the bookshop it is uncertain whether or not this has been intended; at the publisher's it is admitted that the main part of a manuscript has been lost; in a wider context it is explained that part of a book has been banned by the state; at a frontier it happens that the end of a book is confiscated by the customs. There are falsifications by plagiarists and intelligence agencies; useless insertions by encephalograms and computers.

The aim of all this is that it should be like life. In life, language is used less in a search for truth than for attack or defence: facts are censored, rewritten, pushed down into unconsciousness. The beginnings of the novels that have here survived have little in common, it seems, except that their ten or eleven titles (the last novel has nothing but a title) themselves form – guess! – a story or short novel: *If on a winter's night a traveller / Outside the town of Malbork / Leaning from the steep slope / Without fear of wind or vertigo / Looks down in a gathering shadow / In a network of lines that enlace / In a network of lines that intersect / On the carpet of leaves illuminated by the moon / Around an empty grave / What story down there awaits its end? / He asks, anxious to hear the story.*

In between these fragments, which by virtue of their names make up a whole, there are chapters which describe the efforts of a Reader, or Readers, to make sense. The aim of this, again, is to be like life. And by being life-like it is somehow fulfilling: 'reading is a discontinuous and fragmentary operation': however – 'every new book I read comes to be part of that overall and unitary book that is the sum of my readings'. The unifying experience is the relationship between reader and author; between a person and the forces that come to him from outside him. And what is left at the end is in the shape of learning. This process is also like making love. 'Lovers' reading of each other's bodies (of that concentrate of mind and body which lovers use to go to bed together) differs from the reading of written pages in that it is not linear. It starts at any point, skips, repeats itself, goes backward, insists, ramifies in simultaneous and divergent messages, converges again, has moments of irritation, turns the page, finds its place, gets lost.' In this sort of learning which is to do with exposing rather than protecting oneself 'we measure ourselves against something else that is not present, something else that belongs to the immaterial, invisible world.'

This book is a heroic attempt to describe what being conscious is actually like, rather than how we might prefer it to be. The difficulty is, inevitably, that if it is true that what we have come to like about reading is its falsification through linear narrative, then how is something to be made pleasantly readable that aims at being true? For all its wit and cleverness, *If on a winter's night a traveller* may not seduce many of the unconverted into a care for metaphysics: the beginnings of the stories themselves are not sufficiently dramatic, and one feels this might be different. But for those interested in ways of considering and describing experience, the book is a rare treat. 'The lives of individuals of the human race form a constant plot, in which every attempt to isolate one piece of living that has a meaning separate from the rest – for example, the meeting of two people which will become decisive for both – must bear in mind that each of the two brings with himself a texture of events, environments, other people; and from the meeting, in turn, other stories will be derived which will break off from the common story'.

But the invitation is not just to learn about things as they are; it is also to learn about learning – that almost wordless standing-back-from-oneself, being beside oneself, that is like love. At the very end of the book two of the Readers who have been searching with apparent lack of success for the continuation of their stories find themselves in bed together: in this sense, they have come to some temporary happy end. One says: 'Turn off your light: aren't you tired of reading?' The other says: 'Just a moment, I've almost finished *If on a winter's night a traveller* by Italo Calvino'.

Listener, 1981

The Philosopher Fails – The Artist Succeeds

The Philosopher's Pupil. By Iris Murdoch

Iris Murdoch is a professional philosopher, and it has been interesting (though perhaps hitherto somewhat unprofitable) to speculate on what might be the relation between her philosophy and her highly skilful though sometimes weirdly anarchic novelist's art. However in this novel (her twenty-first) she has as her central character a renowned philosopher called Rozanov, and there are deliberate, though still enigmatic, connections made between philosophy and art.

Rozanov returns in his old age to his home town of Ennistone – a spa in the south of England noted for its hot water springs. Rozanov has lost his faith in the efficacy of philosophy, as a priest might have lost his belief in God. (There is in fact such a priest in the novel, Father Bernard, who ends up preaching to the birds about the non-existence of God.) Rozanov converses with Father Bernard: 'You see, the suspicion that one is not only not telling the truth but cannot tell it – that is damnation'. And: 'There isn't any deep structure in the world. At bottom, which isn't very far down, it's all rubble, jumble'.

Rozanov tries to organise the world around him by will: he has a hypnotic effect on people just because, perhaps, he believes there is nothing to be trusted except will. Around him circulate typical Iris Murdoch characters in various states of exaltation or despair: there is the McCaffrey family of a mother and three sons; their wives, servants and girlfriends; all are more or less under the guru-like spell of Rozanov. From their seemingly arbitrary circuits, like those of electrons, there from time to time appear emanations, or portents, such as there often are in Iris Murdoch novels: George McCaffrey glimpses himself walking in the street, flying saucers are seen above a primitive circle of stones; foxes come out of their holes and gambol on lawns; one goes so far as to sit in the front seat of a Rolls-Royce. The hot waters of the spa – the pipes controlling which go down like a colossal organ into the earth – suddenly erupt from a trickle into a geyser. Citizens realise that the town is going through one of its 'funny times': it is as if Tunbridge Wells had been transported to the edge of an animistic rain-forest.

The various strands of passion and hopeless attempts at manipulation whirl fascinatingly enough, even if there is not quite the concentrated, gripping narrative of the same author's *The Black Prince* or *A Word Child*. At the beginning, George McCaffrey tries to murder his wife, then at once dramatically rescues her; at the end he tries to find liberation by murdering Rozanov, but Rozanov happens to be already dead. Tom McCaffrey begins with a boyfriend called Emma and ends married to Rozanov's granddaughter Hattie; he seems to have made this progress through a series of misfortunes. Rozanov himself has a passion for his granddaughter, but common sense and morality suggest he should use his will to give her up. As if to sum up the haphazardness of all this Father Bernard preaches to his birds: 'Metaphysics and the human sciences are made impossible by the penetration of morality into the moment-to-moment conduct of ordinary life; the understanding of this fact is religion'. Most of the characters end up in a trance-like state not very different from that in which they began. Father Bernard at least survives: Rozanov does not. But the chief interest of the novel remains in the question – what is a philosopher making with or from all this?

In her Romanes Lectures of 1976 Iris Murdoch considered the question of why Plato wanted to banish artists from his Republic: artists were apt to dramatise and thus make attractive human stupidity and wickedness and thus were dangerous to an orderly society. In the published version of these lectures, *The Fire and the Sun*, Iris Murdoch seems to agree with Plato's analysis of the situation but then comes down (herself somewhat arbitrarily) against his suggestions about dealing with it: after all, art is about 'the pilgrimage from appearance to reality' ; 'learning an art is . . . learning how to make a formal utterance of a perceived truth'. In *The Philosopher's Pupil* Rozanov says he agrees with Plato ('art is certainly the devil's work') and does not move on from this. He sees that 'the holy must try to know the demonic, must at some point frame the riddle and thirst for the answer'; but nevertheless, he decides that this 'longing is the perfect contradiction of the love of God'. Rozanov's God is a philosopher's god; it cannot live with contradictions.

At some stage in most Iris Murdoch novels there is apt to come to a reader the thought – But surely human beings are not like this:

we do not really, do we, spend our time whirled around by such portent-laden passions imagining we find meanings where there are none? But on the heels of this comes the feeling – Perhaps this is just what human beings are in fact like, and it is precisely our delusion to imagine that we are not. But still there is the further question – What then is this luminously meaningful business of Iris Murdoch writing such intelligent novels, and ourselves getting such pleasure in being informed by them?

The story of *The Philosopher's Pupil* is told by a mysterious narrator, N, who pops up every now and then like one of the portents such as the fox who sits in the front seat of the Rolls-Royce. N describes himself as 'an observer, a student of human nature, a moralist, a man'; it is his 'role in life to listen to stories'. He adds: 'I also had the assistance of a certain lady'. The lady is, it seems, Iris Murdoch. As far as the business of making a formal utterance of a perceived truth goes, it is the philosopher, Rozanov, who, striving for order on a rational and human level, fails; and it is the artist, the writer (the philosopher's pupil?) who, by making out of human disorderliness something orderly on what Father Bernard would call a religious level, succeeds. The artist's achievement is, paradoxically, through listening and observing, to frame and make acceptable not so much answers as riddles.

Listener, 1983

Bits of Gold

The Destinies of Darcy Dancer, Gentleman. By J. P. Donleavy

It is difficult to write a life-affirming novel nowadays: too much is known about the tawdriness and shams of almost all levels of society, and a novel that does not have a social context is in danger of exposing itself to the sterilising rays of subjectivity. It is J. P. Donleavy's achievement to have created both a style of writing and a subject-matter that are in exuberant praise of life, and yet not so fantastical as to seem untrue.

Darcy Dancer, gentleman, is the illegitimate but legal heir to a large estate: his mother dies when he is young, and his inheritance is threatened by the pillages of his appalling non-father. He grows up in a world of drunken butlers, randy grooms, Latin-quoting gardeners, copulating huntsmen, and stunningly lascivious German housekeepers. The setting is Ireland, about which there is a literary tradition, indeed, that such extravagant characterisation might seem true. It is the Ireland of the early and happy chapters of Joyce's *Ulysses*; of Synge's *The Playboy of the Western World*. Darcy Dancer, while still in his teens, manages to escape from and put to rout the predators that surround him; so that he saves, if not quite his inheritance, his dignity and his soul.

The word 'gentleman' is used deliberately and often as an appendage to him: it refers to a style of attitude and behaviour. Darcy Dancer is a bounder – even, at moments, a liar and a cheat. But because he knows he has to be all of these things to survive in a society that is brutal and ravenous, he is also, from this further point of knowing as it were, none of these things: his honest view of himself as reluctantly but necessarily a rogue gives him a skill and an authority. He is a 'dancer' in that he walks on a tightrope with a drop into communal inanity on one side and into his own potential rage on the other: he is a 'trickster' such as is depicted in fairy tales and in Jungian psychology – someone whose honourable duty it is to keep one jump ahead of the tricky ways of the world. Above all, he is brave: and in being all this, he is perhaps doing the best, it is suggested, that a young man can do.

J. P. Donleavy's last book was the extremely funny *The Unexpurgated Code: A Complete Manual of Survival and Manners:* this new novel is an even funnier (and much more touching) illustration of this code. It is picaresque in that it rambles on in the manner of some eighteenth-century novel about rogues: sometimes its extravagances drop over into the realm of parody. But what seem truly and uniquely life-affirming about it are the connections that exist between the story, the style, and what life seems to be about.

In Donleavy's writing there is an almost magically potent blend of the vulgar and the elegant, the grotesque and the lyrical, the archaic and the lewdly up-to-date. The vulgarity is part of the stuff of life: what is also part of life is the elegance and nobility with which human beings can, sometimes, handle the other, darker part – can come to terms with it and even love it. These opposites are held together in Donleavy's writing in the person of the narrator in a quite self-conscious way: the narrator writes of himself now in the first person and now in the third – as if he were naturally aware of himself as in part foolish and helpless, and in part detached from this and with some possibilities of control. His sentences, his repartee, in the way they bring the vulgar and the elegant together, are often weirdly witty; as if in this there is authority and potency. Other characters with whom Donleavy has sympathy come to talk in his style: it is as if life-affirmation were held in an elaborate network the hallmark of which is wit.

There is a marvellous scene in which Darcy Dancer is posing in the nude for a rapacious female painter; he keeps on getting an erection which, so the painter says, spoils the aesthetic line of his pose. So they discuss, and decide, with elaborate courtesy, what is the sensible but otherwise possibly improper thing to do about this: for – 'Dear boy, for you to get an erection just as I am about to make masterpieces is an insult to the whole creative concept'. It is in such a witticism as this that Donleavy excels; the bringing together of the ridiculous and the urgently unavoidable.

Donleavy ends each of his chapters with one of those brief four- or six-line poems that have become a hallmark of his writing. These, too, seem to be distillations, like pearls or tears, of the stresses and strains that have gone before. They seem to say – In life there is a lot of dross, yes; there are also small bits of gold and diamond which, if you find them, are worth more than all the rest put together.

Lament for Lost Childhood

Vladimir Nabokov: A Tribute. Edited by Peter Quennell

This set of essays on Nabokov is much more interesting than most tributes of the kind, since there is an intriguing pattern of argument in spite of the apparent randomness of the points of view – a fact that would have interested the book's subject, Nabokov, and indeed the kind of thing that much of the argument is about. Peter Quennell writes of Nabokov's insistence that the value of a work of art resides in the liveliness of its details: suggestions of 'meanings' or 'messages' were anathema to him. John Bayley agrees about Nabokov's claim that literature should not be seen as 'standing for' anything of importance 'in the history of human consciousness', and should just provoke in the reader a 'purr of beatitude'; but he points out that this in itself contains some vital message about form and content in human consciousness – that 'in all great art the message is dissolved in the beatitude'.

Alex de Jonge suggests that however much Nabokov protested he was not interested in meanings, his books are in fact permeated by patterning, and it is this manipulation of details with their complex repetitions and connections that demonstrates that 'the world is indeed planned and meaningful and not random and haphazard'. Martin Amis begins by decrying such speculation, and says that what is central to Nabokov is just that he spins a jolly good yarn – that it is for his skill in telling stories of 'murder, adultery, obsession and per-verse love' that he should be 'rescued for the mainstream' of European literature. But such is Nabokov's complexity that even Martin Amis is driven later to a subtle speculation – which is that Nabokov must have known that 'art, by celebrating suffering, also domesticates it: "Art is a lie," said Tolstoy: Nabokov would cheerfully agree – hence the innocuously rolling agonies. . . .'

Mark Lilley goes on from this to the idea of Nabokov's art as a sort of therapeutic joke: Nabokov 'creates out of the confusion between the real and the unreal his own delightfully enchanting world of creative deception'. This world is a game without relevance to anything outside: but since it seems to be in the nature of human consciousness to need some such play for mental health, then Nabokov's games might, after all, exercise 'a benign influence on a reader's mind' and thus have 'a *utile* component after all'. We are here back at the beginning with a denial of explicit messages, but having picked up a riddle, a paradox, on the way – which is that however much a work of art is just itself and without further meaning, yet the fact of its appreciation seems to represent something vital about the working of human minds, and so in this sense it does have a meaning.

There have been several nagging occurrences in the course of this journey when an outside reality does seem to be breaking into the descriptions of make-believe worlds. One is John Bayley's insight into *Lolita*. *Lolita* has been taken to be a story about love: John Bayley points out that it is more a story about power. There is a key moment when Lolita, having been told of her mother's death, comes sobbing at night into Humbert's room just because she is an orphan; she has 'nowhere else to go'. Nabokov himself places this phrase deliberately in the centre of the book: it is as if he were saying: 'The delights I am describing are too complex to be those of love: of course the delights of power are enigmatic.' Everyone, that is, knows that power corrupts: but almost everyone still yearns for the nastiness of power.

Alex de Jonge and Mark Lilley seem to be saying that the ability to face this paradox might be the point of Nabokov's games. The desire for power is a black joke because even when power is achieved its ecstasies contain also bewilderment and despair: but it might be just the ability to stand back and recognise this that would give someone the chance to glimpse sanity at the point where he is standing.

Towards the end of the book Robert Alter writes of Nabokov's last large-scale work, *Ada,* and says that here he 'moved boldly from a vision of paradise lost to one of paradise regained'. But in *Ada* the reader is still in the hermetic world of 'stay-at-home' senses: the lovers Ada and Van Veen seem to be almost two parts of the same person, or they are an artist and his muse – the paradise is still that enjoyed between Nabokov and his power with words. One is reminded of Frank Kermode's recent *The Genesis of Secrecy* in which he shows how fundamental concepts may have to be presented in riddles: it is in the nature of life and evolution that not everything by everyone should be comprehended and preserved. But a riddle, even such a disquieting one as the one about power, still has a meaning for those who have ears.

But questions remain – why was Nabokov so jokey about his prejudices? Why did he jeer at Freud? Why did he hate the lively cleverness
of Henry James's *What Maisie Knew* – was it when he was imagining
the dead end of *Lolita*? Why would he not give spontaneous interviews,
but insist rather that questions should be submitted beforehand to
which he would return written answers? To this question he gave the
answer – 'I think like a genius, I write like a distinguished author, and
I speak like a child.' But then – as Freud might have said, as Maisie
might have said, as, God knows, Lolita might have said – what on earth
has he got against children? What is disheartening about Nabokov is
not that he had prejudices, but that he had so little desire or ability
to consider them.

It seems that much of his writing, and indeed of his life, might
have been some protest or lament (George Steiner has said this) for
his lost-paradise childhood in Russia. But then, in the end, one finds
oneself loving once more an artist who is so much in love with his
art. All artists have to protect themselves: it is only the very rarest
whose armour, like a cocoon, presages a breaking-out as well as a
holding in.

Listener, 1979

Desire for Delinquency

The Professor of Desire. By Philip Roth

In Philip Roth's new novel David Kepesh, a professor of literature, goes through the motions attendant on being tethered to eroticism. When young he teams up with an enthusiast called Birgitta with whom he enjoys the usual variations of oral and anal sexuality and dreams of becoming her pimp-voyeur. Later, he marries a beauty of the bitch-goddess type who castrates his confidence – she tries to go back, for satisfaction, to her ex-lover who is a gangster in Hong Kong. When the marriage breaks up, Kepesh goes through a period of impotence and despair; he is helped by psychoanalysis. Then he meets a 'good' girl, Claire, with whom he falls in love and has a fine time in bed and spends one idyllic summer: but he knows he will almost certainly leave her within a year, because she does not provide him with the drug as it were to which he has become accustomed, which is the eroticism of stress and torment.

What makes this gloomy book something more than an older, sadder and wiser version of *Portnoy's Complaint* (it is written in Philip Roth's usual limpid, ruefully disarming style) is, I think, the extra dimension brought in by the hero's interest in literature. He lectures on *Anna Karenina*, on *Madame Bovary*, on Chekhov, Kafka and Genet. Looking at his own predicament, which is not to be able to find any driving-force more important than lust, he justifies this to his analyst. He cites *Macbeth* and *Crime and Punishment*; he says: 'Moral delinquency has been on the minds of serious people for a long time now', and 'Wholly harmless types lead rather constricted lives, don't you think?' So that when he is out of his depression and into the arms of his young mistress, still this is what he knows: 'How much longer before I've had a bellyful of wholesome innocence – how long before the lovely blandness of life with Claire begins to cloy, to pall, and I am out there once again, mourning what I've lost, and looking for my way!'

There has been nothing in the literature that he loves and that he teaches that has shown him any model of how life might be desirable as a successfully going concern. The only patterns that he has been taught to respect are those of disillusionment and despair. There is a moment towards the end of the book when he wonders: 'Is the notion of duty so utterly horrendous? . . . Is there not a point on life's way when one yields to duty, welcomes duty as one once yielded to pleasure . . . ?' But he seems to have no equipment in his mind or in his feelings to hold on to such an idea. The book ends with him sucking desperately at the breast of his sleeping mistress and knowing, sensibly enough, that he may not want to go on doing this for ever.

Kepesh never seems able to progress much beyond what Freud called the oral or the anal stage of sexuality – for the most part his sexual activity has to do with sucking, talking, tying, tormenting: there is no sense of the liberation of the self, or the transcendence of the self, that can be found in genital sexuality. Sexuality, to Roth, seems always to be a bondage and not a release: and indeed this is a not unusual experience. But also there is the realisation that this sort of predicament – enslavement – does seem to be a subject of much of world literature: it seems easier to write, and read, stories about helplessness than about freedom. And then there is the even more alarming thought that this also seems to have something to do with a condition of life – it seems easier to live in some sort of enslavement rather than to embark on the hard graft towards release. In enslavement you know where you are: you are at home, as it were, within the bounds of a comic or tragic story. In freedom, you are apt to be somewhat at sea.

One of the most telling moments in the book is when Claire tells Kepesh that she has become pregnant by him, and that although she adores him and wants to live with him for ever, she has had the child aborted without telling him in order not to impinge on his 'freedom'. Even Kepesh, with his confused ideas about what is or not free, finds this odd. (It is this that drives him to ruminate on the possible pleasures of duty.) But the fact is that Claire has almost as little capacity as Kepesh for the skill and dedication necessary for a good life. What they have both become accustomed to are models of life as something that is naturally aborted (Kepesh's wife, too, 'naturally' has an abortion), because this is how they have been conditioned – even by literature. They can thus be slothful; and with no new life coming in to challenge them they can know exactly, like moribund things, where they are.

Parallels between life and literature do seem apt and ominous here: people love a good story about other people's defeats and helplessness because then they need not feel too badly about their own. Philip Roth illustrates this in his somewhat haphazard, melancholy way. Popular stories in which goodness is successful are reserved for children's books and fantasies. And grown-ups who have learned with difficulty that there is some sort of good life possible have learned perhaps too that they cannot publicise this much; there are powerful conventional forces, both inside and outside them, to take it away.

Listener, 1978

No Answer from the Sky

Joseph Conrad: The Three Lives. By Frederick R. Karl

The subtitle of this huge and admirable biography refers to Conrad's 'three lives' as a Pole, a sailor and a writer: but one of Frederick Karl's skills is in showing how the loneliness and struggle of one part of Conrad's life led into, and grew out of, another. 'Having lost his mother, then his father, having assimilated in his childhood and youth the idea of a Poland devoured by Russia . . . he chose another emptiness, the sea, a vastitude that could swallow him up. Following that, he focused on still another emptiness, a limitless, open-ended career as a writer, dominated by sheets of white paper whose horizons extended infinitely'. What Conrad – a Pole who only began to speak English when he was twenty – brought to English literature was a sense of the desolation that hangs over much of human life outside the protections of bourgeois provincialism; also, a way of using words that is masculine, muscular – a style like that of a ship, as it were, beating through chaotic seas. Conrad's brilliance as a stylist is connected to his unfamiliarity with his chosen language – to his struggle with it, by which he could show off his strength. But it was also perhaps his sense of never being at ease that made the substance of his stories so often weaken into melodrama.

Conrad came from a family of would-be revolutionaries at a time when there was little hope of revolution: people talked, and were defeated. He learned the destructive power of politics: 'It first seduces, then it discards'. He ran off to Marseilles when he was sixteen; he joined the English mercantile marine; he was a captain before he was thirty. During the changeover period from being a seaman to being a novelist, he went on a journey to the interior of what was then the Belgian Congo. He used this journey later as the stuff of his story *Heart of Darkness*.

The journey and the story were focal points in Conrad's career. In the story there is the feel of magnificent landscapes through which humans flit: the humans for the most part are squalid. They pillage Africa out of some destructiveness in their minds: the darkness is not so much in the world as in the nature of consciousness. Conrad himself wrote: 'What makes mankind tragic is not that they are the victims of nature, it is that they are conscious of it. To be part of the animal kingdom under conditions of this earth is very well – but as soon as you know of your slavery, the pain, the anger, the strife – the tragedy begins'. Frederick Karl comments: 'That tremendous preponderance of death and suicide in Conrad – fifteen suicides alone – is attached . . . to the perhaps deeper theme that actual extinction was the sole way of gaining or understanding life'. The word 'extinction' here is odd: a descent to the depths for understanding, yes; but – extinction?

Lovers of Conrad usually take his central works to be *Heart of Darkness*, *Lord Jim* and *Nostromo*, with *The Secret Agent* and *Under Western Eyes* as powerful whirlpools perhaps slightly off the mainstream. In all these works, the narrative is to do with people in some way cursed – whose curse indeed drives them towards extinction. But what is notably not to do with extinction is the tough, ironic and intellectual style of the narration – by Conrad himself, by the multiple narrators that he brings in like mirrors to reflect and to elaborate himself. The curse is to do with the subject matter – with human life destroying and being destroyed because of both its squalor, and its vulnerability through knowledge. What can stand back from the curse are just the small but resolute voices of individuals and artists talking, talking – weaving their spells against it. But they, at the end – like the Polish revolutionaries; like Ibsen's peeler of onions – are apt to come to nothing.

Throughout Conrad's work (and indeed it seems to me throughout much of European literature) there is this double view of consciousness. On the one hand, consciousness is what forces humans to be aware of chaos and suffering and so denies them the peace-of-mind which (it is presumed) is the prerogative of animals; on the other hand, it is consciousness that can make chaos and suffering appear endurable and even noble, because it can provide an impression of 'meaning' on some higher level of self-reflection, and through works of art. An artist must have some such impression by virtue of his calling: without it, there would be nothing to be distinguished as art. But what writers are apt to portray (and, indeed, often to demonstrate in their daily lives) is life as chaos and suffering quite apart from meaning. It is as if the subject matter of their calling seldom runs in harmony with the hope and wonder with which they pursue it, and the dedication which they put into it. Conrad was an extreme example of this – of both the zest, and the debility.

Throughout his life – except, presumably, when he was being efficient at sea – he suffered from illnesses which now would be called psychosomatic – 'gout, arthritis, delirious fevers, neuralgia, influenza' (Frederick Karl's list). In later life, Conrad and his wife Jessie and his two sons seemed to be 'moving in and out of each other's ailments so that in some form of symbiosis they could survive, paradoxically, by means of their support of each other'. He could not work effectively 'unless he were close to breakdown, on the edge of psychic disorders, ill in body and mind'. It was this that protected him from outside distractions: it also enabled him, from a starting-point of miseries, to embark resolutely towards a heart of darkness. Like this, he could concentrate on his journey; and others could concentrate on him.

Mr Karl is a wise and erudite writer who, in his 900 pages, moves confidently around the shores of literary, historical and psychoanalytical understanding: it is unlikely that there will be a better full-scale biography of Conrad in the foreseeable future. But there is some lack – though perhaps this is outside the terms of a biography – of an attempt to answer the question of what is this curse that so often seems to hang over the minds of writers: the fact that it must be an impression of the possibility of meaning that makes them write, but what so many write about are people and situations laden with inanity and doom.

Conrad used illness to protect himself: as he grew older he became decreasingly fatherly and increasingly dependent childishly on his ill and much younger wife. But still he was successful: he did, brilliantly, write. At the end of his life he was a grand old man of English letters: he had worked dedicatedly and passionately for this. But the people he wrote about made no profitable use of their furies: they were, simply, defeated. Conrad saw that 'our refuge is in stupidity, in drunkenness of all kinds; in lies, in beliefs, in murder, thieving, reforming – in negation, in contempt': what he did not see, and what he seemed to get no satisfaction from even at the end of his life, was the enormous irony, almost joke, of the way in which all these miseries could still be used for the making of something which was recognised as great art.

There is a strange passage from a letter which Mr Karl quotes when Conrad is disclaiming his own reputation: 'I doubt if greatness can be attained now in imaginative prose work: when it comes it will be in a new form; a form for which we are not ripe as yet'. There is a moment in *Heart of Darkness* when a narrator says of the demonic Mr Kurtz:

'There was something wanting in him – some small matter which, when pressing need arose, could not be found under his magnificent eloquence'. It was some such comment that Conrad seemed to be making about himself – about the despair that lay under the magnificent monologues of his prose. Perhaps he saw – as later writers such as Beckett seem to have seen – that simple eloquence, however brilliant, is like a child crying out against the fact of its dependence; against the fate from which, as a child, it cannot be free. But then – what would be the sound that an artist might make who saw that his adult freedom might be in just his ability to see this; and that this ability, however grim his situation, might be recognised as a growing-up?

Conrad's *bête noire* in literature was Dostoevsky – who went as deep into the heart of darkness as Conrad did, but who emerged with some hope and wonder intact. Mr Karl pinpoints the difference: 'Conrad demonstrated his distaste for nearly all human behaviour caught as it was in a senseless universe. For Dostoevsky, sin, even the worst, was a form of energy and tied one to the workings of the universe'. But this is the area that critics do not venture to make many maps of. In Dostoevsky there are people listening as well as talking: the chance of redemption lies in the stuff of humanity and of the universe being the same. Alyosha for instance does not talk much; he lets the talk of other people as it were break over him; and then at the end there are the children who cry: 'Hurrah for Karamazov!' Conrad faced the curse of his childhood; he cried out, magnificently, against a universe that seemed quite alien from him. But there is, in Conrad, little sense of repartee. It is as if, shaking his fist at the sky, he did not want to wait for it to answer. If it had, all sorts of new responsibilities might have come in: such as, perhaps, an inquiry not just into heart of darkness but into the artistry which can make the connections between inquiry and darkness such a joy.

Listener, 1970

Dissidence

Dostoevsky: The Years of Ordeal, 1850-1859. By Joseph Frank

Dostoevsky's life is of great contemporary interest – especially that part of it covered by this volume (the second of a projected five) of Joseph Frank's admirably comprehensive biography. During these years Dostoevsky was arrested as a dissident under the oppressive regime of Tsar Nicholas I, was sentenced to death and reprieved, was exiled to Siberia – for four years in a prison camp and for five in compulsory service in the army. The grounds for his arrest were slight; the staging of a mock execution and the last-minute reprieve were horrific; the years in prison were of extreme brutality and degradation. Yet looking back on this time Dostoevsky said that if he had not been arrested he would have gone mad; it was his previous life as a young radical intellectual that had been destroying him; that what he learned in Siberia was that it was through confrontation with the depths of reality that one experienced hope.

Professor Frank says he has deliberately subordinated Dostoevsky's private life to 'a depiction of his interconnection with the literary and social-cultural history of his time'. It is in this that he is so successful, and his emphasis seems justified. Dostoevsky's personality in the book does seem somewhat in the shadows; but this is where Dostoevsky himself seems to have kept it. With his nondescript, guarded appearance he was an observer, a seer; a mouthpiece of whatever had to be said. He discarded the contemporary literary tradition of 'portrayal of character through incidents linked together by the largely commonplace events of ordinary social existence', and embarked on an inquiry into, and a portrayal of, the religious drama of the redemption of individuals and of society.

Before his arrest he had been involved in the arguments of intellectual politics: it could be seen that society was wrong, so what rationally could be done to put it right? One held meetings, produced papers, formed secret societies; one became intoxicated by the righteousness of one's ideologies. It was this pattern that Dostoevsky came to see as some sort of mental illness: people thought they could alter the world like this only if they did not know what human beings were like.

One of the beliefs of Russian intellectuals in the 1840s had been that Russian peasants as a class held whatever potentialities there were for social goodness; social evil was caused by those who kept them oppressed. Dostoevsky found in prison that Russian peasants had a propensity for evil that he had not before imagined. But because this evil was a reality acted out, and not a delusion barricaded in the mind, it did seem to contain in it paradoxically the seeds of regeneration.

What Dostoevsky learned during his years in prison with the force of a religious conversion was to do with paradoxes: it is through becoming a victim that one can be brought to sanity, it is through physical degradation that one can find dignity, it is only through death and resurrection that there can be development. This seems to be true about individuals; and it seemed to be true, Dostoevsky felt, about Russia. For all his distancing himself from the trivialities of Russian literary life and his hatred for the all-powerful bureaucracy, he saw a special role for Russia in the ordering of the world – perhaps just because in Russia paradoxes were acted out so blatantly, while the rest of the world seemed caged within its delusions.

There are times when the similarities between Dostoevsky's situation during these years and the situations of Russian dissidents today seem so great as to be uncanny: communism, it appears, is only one of the forms like devils and angels that paradoxes take in Russia. There are similarities between Dostoevsky's attitude of mind and that of exiles such as Solzhenitsyn: both are appalled by brutalities within Russia, but both are also appalled by the self-destructive trivialities of so-called Western enlightenment. Both feel that it is out of the squalors of Russia that some sort of resurrection may come, just because the battles going on there are real ones while the power-games of the West often seem simply silly. This is to underrate the liveliness of some styles that have evolved self-consciously from game-playing; but one feels that Dostoevsky would have recognised this had he been a dissident today.

One of Dostoevsky's insights was that although so-called 'strong' characters are the ones who run society, they are also, because they get carried away blindly by their own assurance, apt to defeat their own ends; and it is 'weak' characters, who worry about moral responsibility and meanings in life and death, who, although they are often held in disdain by society, do in fact affect society in the way in which 'strong' characters do not – just because their activities are tempered and thus made effective by what they instinctively understand about paradoxes. Good writers, I suppose, in this sense are 'weak' characters. But it is their work that lives and breeds in the world's consciousness.

Listener, 1984

'The New Humanism Is Coming, in Spite of All the Barbarism'

The Thomas Mann Diaries. Selected by Hermann Kesten

Thomas Mann began to keep diaries when he was a schoolboy in the 1890s; he burned them all in 1945 except ones between 1918 and 1921, which he had set aside for background material for his novels; also ones from 1933 on, which he put in a sealed packet marked 'of no literary value' and with the instruction that they were not to be opened until twenty years after his death. This 350-page selection from what has survived may not be of 'literary value' in that it consists of jottings of day-to-day events and stray thoughts in a flat style; but as a record of how, from just such basic material, a writer can build two or three masterpieces of European literature, it is of great human interest.

Between 1918 and 1921 Thomas Mann lived in Munich. In the aftermath of war right-wing gangs fought left-wing gangs in the streets; a revolutionary government briefly came to power; there were shortages of food and fuel, and often postal services and public transport did not work. Mann lamented the passing of old and customary forms of order, and he poured scorn on the hypocrisies of the new style of politics. He noted that 'one mob is the same as another' and that 'fundamentally, what is human is alien to politics'. Off-stage, as it were, from the haphazard and melodramatic events being observed, such thoughts were being transmuted into the luminous orderliness of *The Magic Mountain*.

The Magic Mountain tells of the almost wilfully self-inflicted collapse of the old Europe; it ends with the debacle but also possible purgation of the First World War. At a central point of the story the hero, Hans Castorp, has a dream in which he sees beautiful human beings walking hand-in-hand on a beach: their harmony seems to depend on their recognition of what is going on in a nearby temple, where hideous hags are ritualistically dismembering a child. Hans Castorp thinks: 'The recklessness of death is in life . . . from love and sweetness alone can form come . . . always in silent recognition of the blood sacrifice'.

In Munich, Thomas Mann went to a performance of *Parsifal* and recorded how he felt 'at home' in its 'aura of sickness' – in the 'compound of religious impulse, sheer lasciviousness, and sure-handed competence that comes across as wisdom'.

In March 1933, he and his wife Katia were on holiday in Switzerland; the Reichstag had just been burned down and Hitler had assumed dictatorial powers; the Manns were warned by their children that they should not return to Munich, where they would probably be arrested for what were already well known to be his anti-Nazi views. Thomas Mann was one of the first to see that the appeal of Nazism was due not so much to the sort of dynamism that it professed, as to some sort of spiritual vacuum into which people were drawn because there they could feel absolved from responsibility. His comments on the daily brutalities become ever more laconic: 'revolting', 'horrible and base'. He has only occasionally 'secret, disquieting musings' that some cleansing may come out of the destruction. For the most part there is in evidence just 'the hatred of the simple-minded for any form of subtlety, which they feel to be antinational and galling to the point of arousing murderous rage'.

During these years he was writing *Joseph in Egypt*, in which is told the story of Joseph being carried off as a slave to a strange land; nevertheless when he is there, by a process both of cunning and of acceptance of his fate, Joseph achieves a position of the highest influence; he does this because he believes in a God who has plans for him, which he himself can aid by 'a mingling of calculation and sincerity'. Joseph is 'the first person in the world' to break away from the traps of primitive patterns of mind and to experience 'liberality of thought'. By having a sense of personal destiny, he feels free to stand back from himself and observe what God has in store.

After 1933, the Manns did not go back to Germany; they settled at first in Zurich and then in America, where in 1938 and 1939 Thomas Mann went on lecture tours. In the diaries are recorded the fears and tribulations of being in strange lands. Hitler invades the Rhineland, Austria, Czechoslovakia; there is the impression of Mann being pursued by furies; one day, there might be nowhere further to go. Nevertheless he becomes a champion in the struggle against Hitler by his outspokenness. His U.S. publisher tells him: 'You are Hitler's most formidable enemy.'

During the last three years of the 1930s Thomas Mann wrote *Lotte in Weimar* in which there is successfully depicted – largely through the imagined vision of another writer of genius, Goethe – the sort of orderliness and foundation on which a life of the spirit can thrive. Goethe is an old man; he fusses about his daily routines and his duties at court; in his head there flower miraculous constructions to do with life, science, art. Goethe explains to his one-time love, Lotte: 'Know that metamorphosis is all that is dearest and innermost of thy friend . . . unity in change and flux, conversion constant out of and into oneself'. Thomas Mann travels to and fro, moves his home, loses his possessions and finds them again; he records his exhaustions, his depressions, his toothaches. He goes for his morning or his afternoon walk, and is aware of the sun and the sea: sometimes there is the vision of a young man who arouses a sensuous wonder in him that is different from, though intertwined with, his love of his wife and his five children. He continues to watch in the world of politics 'the spiteful satisfaction people get in the failure of things'; he never loses his belief that 'at the same time the more or less conscious desires of mankind are none the less fulfilled in due course'.

These diaries may not mean much to those without any knowledge or love of Mann's work: to others they are likely to spark off lively and potent reflections. Throughout the best part of his life Thomas Mann seemed to be saying that just out of the humdrum mankind can create, in co-operation with the divine, something of extraordinary luminousness and power. And this is not a prerogative only of the artist, but of everyone who 'opens wide his eyes upon the unity of the world'.

Thomas Mann, like Goethe, did not see art, or what goes on in the mind, as something separate from the way the world works; he thought it was the proper function of humans to recognise this and to intertwine the one with the other. In *Lotte in Weimar*, Goethe ruminates upon his theories about plants, colour, light. Thomas Mann, in 1934, just after Hitler's murder of the stormtrooper leader Röhm, is talking to a poet friend who tells him of the 'new and all-important work in theoretical physics, its new image of the world in the cosmos, thanks to which revised concept man emerges with a strange new sovereignty'. Thomas Mann comments –

> I at once understood that this has to be seen in conjunction with the new anthropology, with the entire new science of man, for taken together these would provide the foundation of the new humanism that is coming into being in the best minds in spite of all the barbarism.

Listener, 1983

Against the Tyranny of Genes

Arthur Koestler: The Homeless Mind. By David Cesarani

Koestler was a towering literary figure in my youth in the '40s and '50s. It was from his books that I and others learned why people became communists and then stopped being communists (*Arrow in the Blue: The God That Failed*): why faithful Stalinists confessed to crimes they had never committed (*Darkness at Noon*): how a passionate Zionist could come to turn against Zionism (*Thieves in the Night: Promise and Fulfillment*). It was even from an early pot-boiler of which he was a pseudonymous co-author, *Encyclopaedia of Sexual Knowledge,* that as a schoolboy one quarried bizarre aspects of sex.

Later there were the autobiographical books written from the heart of the tumultuous events of the mid-century. Then came finally the would-be scientific books of the '60s and '70s that passionately argued the case against behaviourism and reductionism, and aimed to endow with intellectual respectability what Koestler called 'holism' and even the paranormal.

David Cesarani has written a long and detailed book that is good about the early politics and history, but has less sympathy with the later science and conjectures, and is too repetitive about the social junketing. He says his main theme has been to reinstate at the centre of the story Koestler's 'Jewish identity' (Cesarani's previous publications have been concerned with the Holocaust). But the results of this aim are enigmatic.

Koestler, by birth a Hungarian Jew, spent his last thirty years mainly in England. He went to the newly created state of Israel in 1948 committed to helping in its battle for survival. After some months there he turned against the way in which Zionism was evolving, also against conventional concepts of Jewishness. Such dramatic *volte-faces*, as with his communism, seemed part of his nature: but he felt strongly that a powerful and rigid Rabbinical Judaism would store up political trouble for Israel, and that in the *Diaspora* the preservation of Jewish separateness would perpetuate anti-Semitism. He went to emphatic lengths to renounce his own Jewishness; but it is Mr Cesarani's claim that he found it impossible to carry this through, in that he was never able to accept any country as his home.

For all his intellectual brilliance and charm, Koestler was, in Cesarani's account, an unpleasant man – a bully, a frequent drunk, a sometimes brutal sexual predator. But his three wives adored him, and his friends were enthralled by him, and behaviour amongst intellectuals in the post-war '50s was apt to be more ragged than in this primly snooping age. And Koestler's ambivalence about politics, and about his Jewishness, was an extension of the way in which he saw individuals and himself. In his would-be scientific books he contended that humans suffered from a fault in their genetic make-up; it was this that made them aggressive and self-destructive, and this that would have to be looked at before politics and society could be improved. Until such a time as when genetic engineering might be feasible, humans should therefore address themselves to a 'vertical' as well as to a 'horizontal' dimension – to the way in which the specifically human ability to recognise art, humour, and a religious 'oceanic feeling', might temper animal-like struggles for power.

Koestler was at pains not to see this as mysticism, and he tried to argue his case against neo-Darwinist determinists rationally – to propose that there was a scientific basis for believing that evolution had some system of patterning that humans might be privy to. But this was difficult to put into scientific words, and these were days in which battle-lines between scientists and so-called creationists were drawn simply; and in his late forays towards and into the paranormal Koestler invited, and received, a certain ridicule. But it is striking that a hard-headed neo-Darwinist, Richard Dawkins, would soon (1976) be writing at the end of his hugely influential *The Selfish Gene* – 'We are built as gene machines . . . but . . . we alone on earth can rebel against the tyranny of the selfish replicators' – and one feels that these words might have been written by Koestler in his heyday.

At the end of his life, plagued with Parkinson's disease and leukemia, Koestler – a vice-president of the Euthanasia Society – committed suicide, in which his dedicated wife Cynthia had agreed to join him. This event too brought obloquy on him. But it was part of his belief that the time had come for humans to take more charge of their destiny; and in a matter of life and death, as in that of Jewishness, why should not a stand be taken against the tyranny of genes?

Daily Telegraph, 1998

Jerusalem: A Novel of Hope that Cannot Find a Publisher

Jerusalem: A Postsexual Narrative. By Eric Mace-Tessler

This novel is daring in form, packed with explicit and implicit meaning, and – just when the complexities of the printed page might seem to be daunting – so engrossing that except for brief and necessary breathing-spaces it is difficult to put down. Any one of such attributes is rare in a modern novel; for them to occur all at once in a work by a hitherto (and still) unpublished author is an event of the highest artistic significance.

The story concerns the spiritual and material journey of David Siegfried, a Jew brought up in Brooklyn in the 1950s and '60s. He becomes a student in London in the 1970s, a teacher of history and literature in Basel in the '80s and '90s, and goes on a pilgrimage down the Rhine to visit his family's home-town of Worms just after the turn of the millennium. The childhood years are described in an austerely classical style as might befit a haunted and restricted Jewish upbringing; liberation in London is told in a more comic and ironic vein suited to the pragmatic English environment; the third part, when David is a professor, is narrated in the punning and allusive literary style of someone well aware of the self-conscious forces and fashions of modernism. Then in the fourth part, the most complex and dazzlingly illuminating part of the book, there is a virtuoso display of profundity in the form of what is all too often a superficial post-modernist conceit – the idea that the import of a text is dependent on the observations of commentators. The author here takes up the challenge of this pretension and uses it for his own creative purposes. On the printed page, that is, around David Siegfried's narrative poem describing his climactic journey, which is printed centrally, there are surrounding columns of commentaries on the events that occur to him and his family both by people who play a part in David's life, and by those who might be academics. It is this format that at first sight seems forbidding. But a reader quickly gets used to the style required for reading – the central poem first, then the columns of commentary in due order – and then an experience is provided which, it seems to me, is unique in literature. It is as if the progenitors of, and participants in, the teutonically epic poem are engaged, as part of what is necessary for their own understanding, in some Talmudic commentary on it; so that what is offered to the reader is the chance to take this in all at once together with his own conjectures – regarding both the narrative and the host of ramifications from it – which endows him with a vision of totality that is breathtakingly beyond the scope of the customary use of words. It is as if he has been invited, and has accepted the invitation, to be part of this creation.

David Siegfried is brought up in a New York Jewish community that is haunted by the Holocaust – members of his family have been lost in the death-camps. This haunting is understandable and yet deadening: the present has become a slave to the past. As a child David tries fancifully to set a trap for the past: to capture it and disarm it, so that he himself may be free of it.

His liberation in London is social and sexual: but still – are not the power-drives inherent in social manoeuvring and sexuality the forces that cause so much human oppression and suffering? David does not feel at home in the lack of spiritual curiosity in England. But then – either with or without alliance to conventional power-drives – where does a Jew feel peacefully at home?

In Basel, David has a Swiss wife, Hannah-Marie, and a daughter, Vera. In the physical world some liberation from the past has been achieved, but the spiritual still seems a prey to the social and sexual. David lectures on the near-impossibility of escaping from the determining forces of history: there are the powers of imagination, but how can imagination affect actuality? Hannah-Marie remembers a key sentence of David's – 'Redemption can only be achieved by liberating and intensifying the bodily senses, and by attaining and sustaining that mode of vision that does not cancel the fallen world, but transfigures it, revealing the lineaments of its eternal imaginative form.' But what does this portend – that lineaments of imagination may be in the outside world?

In the fourth part of the book – that concerned with the family's journey to Worms – the connections and allusions come in so fast and piercingly that they do seem to belong to an external world – some network that is there for the imagination to make use of, if recognised. The reader himself becomes involved in a search, a process of enlightenment; one in which the matter of the printed page seems to be being transformed into inner energy. The reader seems to be learning, like David Siegfried, the objectively creative possibilities of his own mind.

On their arrival in Worms David and Hannah and their daughter Vera go to visit the old Jewish synagogue which was destroyed by the Nazis and is now rebuilt. There Vera, aged eighteen, is abducted by a gang of neo-Nazis and threatened with rape; the abductors see however the more profitable possibility of acquiring a ransom from her father. David comprehends that in order to rescue his daughter he has to go on some spiritual as well as physical journey – force is not effectively countered simply by force. He insists, strangely, that his wife Hannah leave him and return home: father and daughter have to learn to deal with their responsibilities for their predicament on their own – as Jews, and in their relationship as parent and child. For this, David goes on some journey into the dark, to discover the roots of as it were his own abduction and entrapment by the history of his race. This is the most uncanny and portentous part of the book. David realises that if he searches for Vera rationally and directly he will not find her: he has to discover what lineaments there are to be trusted in the outside world. Only thus will he have a chance of rescuing his daughter Vera, or Truth.

He comes across coincidences that tempt him, or guide him, on his way; he finds unlikely helpers. When he does reach Vera in the hands of her captors he still does not engage in direct and futile battle; he does not plead, nor invoke sweet reason; instead he holds up a mirror as it were to the Nazis so that they can glimpse themselves: he does this by telling them a story. And then he leaves Vera, now perhaps armed to fight her own battles. This she succeeds in doing – partly by resolute resistance, partly by the manoeuvre of suddenly appearing to be yielding so that her enemies are thrown off balance, and on account of their pride in their own delusions allow her to get away. Thus by the use of imagination, of subtlety in the face of complexity, Vera is reunited with her family. It is almost impossible to describe how in this part of the book the author effectively gets away with it, but he does. And the reader is left bathed in a shower of what might be his own possibilities.

Central to the book is the idea that humans need not be paralysed by impositions from the past; there is enough in history to recon- struct what we wish for the present. It is often easier to choose to be trapped by the past: freedom is daunting. We have to try not to be subservient to nor to obliterate the fallen world, but to transfigure it: not to batter our heads against the brick walls of evil, but to watch and listen to find a way through; and then this might appear as if it were in partnership with the lineaments of our imagination. Such an experience may indeed be just beyond the scope of words; but words can offer occasions for it.

Jerusalem is a story about a Jew, but Jews have always properly been seen as representatives of all humanity. The evil done to Jews is the haunting and paralysing ghost of this century: the preservation or destruction of Jerusalem is the symbol of the predicament, or choice, that faces humanity in the millennium. Either we continue to be content to see ourselves as unreconstructed murderers and victims, or we learn, from light generated within us on our journey, to use the creative possibilities that emerge from darkness and adversity.

Introduction to *Jerusalem: A Postsexual Narrative*, 1977

Gilbert Sorrentino and *Mulligan Stew*

Nietzsche wrote in 1889 –

> Language belongs in its origins to the age of the most rudimentary form of psychology: we find ourselves in the midst of a rude fetishism when we call to mind the basic presuppositions of the metaphysics of language – which is to say, of *reason*. It is *this* which sees everywhere deed and doer; this which believes in will as cause in general; this which believes in the 'ego', in the ego as being, in the ego as substance, and which projects its belief in the ego-substance on to all things.

Ever since the time of Nietzsche writers who try to describe what life is actually like, rather than feed the illusions of people who want to have illusions, have found themselves facing the sort of predicament outlined by Nietzsche – the predicament that language, the stuff of their trade, has for the most part been used to fortify mental defence-works, and that an attempt to describe experience accurately has to become involved in attacking these defence-works before it can properly (if ever) describe new structures. 'Creative' writing has become a matter of describing the processes of destruction and the vision of creativity itself: too much assumption of a resulting 'structure' is suspect because it might be a defence-work.

The first book of Gilbert Sorrentino's that I read was *Imaginative Qualities of Actual Things*. In this the fortunes of a number of characters were described for the most part conventionally; then the author would break in to tell his readers that they must remember, if they were to be interested in what was going on truly, that of course his characters did not exist, they were created by him, and it was only by a reader's realisation of this that he or she would not be trapped in illusion. But still, a reader might justifiably ask, what in fact was going on? what was the non-illusion that the author cared about so much that he should take such trouble to tell his readers they should not be trapped in illusion.

I don't think that in *Imaginative Qualities of Actual Things* Gilbert Sorrentino quite gave an answer to this: some answer was there, but it did not seem represented by the book. In a sense the book was too simple: it was like a game of skittles in which characters were set up to be knocked down. But *Mulligan Stew*, the only other book of Gilbert Sorrentino's I have read, is not simple: there is a sense of urgency about it like machine-gun fire. The sort of message that comes through is – either you, the readers, see that almost all your conventional ways of seeing things, reading about things, writing about things, are parodies; or you yourself will evaporate into a sort of parody yourself.

In *Mulligan Stew* Gilbert Sorrentino is writing a novel about a novelist writing a novel in which the characters become also characters in Gilbert Sorrentino's novel and as such they stand back from and criticise the man who is writing them. The ways in which this is done become almost totally matters of parody, often extremely funny, in which people, or characters, step out not only from their contexts, but from the styles in which the contexts might conventionally be described – in order to laugh at them. It is as if Gilbert Sorrentino were saying – this is the best way to describe life: literature has become a parody of life, so if we parody literature might we not be getting close to life: only thus might we not be trapped in novelettish illusions. As Nietzsche, again, said – 'Objection, evasion, happy distrust, pleasure in mockery are signs of health: everything unconditional belongs to pathology'.

More and more as I read *Mulligan Stew* I was reminded of Nietzsche: my admiration for Sorrentino became my admiration for someone with the courage to face built-in paradoxical predicaments and not to be got down by these. Conventional writing not only ignores questions of what is a projected illusion and what is not, but by so doing drugs and deadens its readers: it turns people into junkies by making a junk of life. There is almost no conventional writing that does not, unless it is self-consciously a fairy-story, make out life to be squalid or absurd, but in such a style that people get comfort from this. It is an extraordinary comment that a writer has to appear 'experimental' if he is to show any zest for life. Gilbert Sorrentino has enormous zest: he may be saying that life is absurd, but from such a fierce standpoint that it is impossible to feel that this standpoint is absurd. *Mulligan Stew*, for all its complexity, is a more enjoyable book than the earlier and easier one.

The problem is, as always, how to make an artwork of all this: how to communicate in writing the realisation that writing has conventionally become a purveyor of lies, but that this realisation is truthful. Parody does have a function here: but at the centre of this there should be a touch of authenticity. I think this can be *felt* in *Mulligan Stew,* but it is not *described.* When, reading the book, I was under its bombardment of jokes, allusions, images, what I needed from time to time was some glimpse of where the firing was coming from: I would turn to the back flap of the dust jacket and would look at the photograph of Gilbert Sorrentino himself as he sat in some workroom, kitchen, bedroom, or whatever, and looked out furiously on to his bemused world. Thus reassured, I would go back to the text. The personal image seemed a thread of authenticity through the maze.

Some people will find from their own interests a thread: most will not; so either an unconventional writer will lose such readers, or else he will have to provide something of his own threads for them as well as his maze. This is difficult. The business of trying to describe the actual mazes of life is different from the business of oneself trying to find ways through them: or even if this is not so (there are paradoxes here) however clearly the maze can be presented by a writer, the thread has always to some extent to be found by a person on his own. A second-hand thread is not a true one. But there can conceivably be, in a book, hints about thread-making as it were. Gilbert Sorrentino stimulates visions of these: perhaps to ask for something more definite is to court illusion.

I was reminded of Faulkner's *The Sound and the Fury* in which, after pages of turmoil, the reader is offered the chance of a sudden illuminating flash in which he can see the pattern of the whole. This is provided partly by the spaced-out structure of the story – the same events are descried by different characters at different times so that by this setting-up of polarities, as it were, the reader can achieve his own spark of understanding: but there is also a conventional doom-and-damnation element to the story on which it is easy perhaps for a reader to strike his own match of recognition. This element is one that Gilbert Sorrentino is parodying, so its conventional use is not available to him. But he does provide spacing and structure.

It seems to me that there still might thus be some representation of 'signs of health' (Nietzsche's words) through styles of 'happy distrust' and 'pleasure in mockery', however difficult it is to describe health except in terms of recognition of disease – hence parody. A description of health would have to remain a bit secret, perhaps; or iconoclasts might smash it; or one's own infantile yearnings might make an illusion of it. But there are a lot of profoundly interesting things going on in the worlds of scientific enquiry and enquiry into ideas – and on just such a subject as the way in which reality can perhaps best be described in terms of what might be called parodies. But this realisation itself contains much energy. What there might be here is some cross-fertilisation from a structure of spaced-out contexts – imaginative and heuristic. 'Creative' writers have at the moment the energy to create their parodies: Gilbert Sorrentino is ebulliently and furiously aware of what he is doing: it is about his threading his way through his awareness that there might be a further authenticity.

Review of Contemporary Fiction, 1981

Part III
Pathology and Sanity

On a dark night a person searches on the brightly lit ground under a lamp-post. A passerby asks – For what are you searching? The person says – For the keys to my house. The passerby says – Is this where you lost them? The person says – No I lost them in the dark, but this is where the light is.

From *Journey into the Dark*, II

One of the consequences of a realisation that there are no lost keys beneath a lamp-post – together with the insistence that there is still no sense in moving out of the circle of light – was the literary pretension known as deconstruction – the contention that in literature there is no sense in searching for an author's meaning nor indeed for any meaning that might be called authentic; a critic can give to a text whatever interpretation he or she likes. Authors, it was supposed, are at the mercy of their social or psychological predispositions; they cannot, since these are unconscious, be aware of these themselves; critics however can – and can sport with them under the light. It can of course be said that critics are at the mercy of their social and psychological predispositions, but such a contention would be part of the game – the lumbering game in which there is no claim to authenticity but just the spectacle of academics leaping and scoring points by popping balls through hoops. This might seem an interesting occupation for a time, but then onlookers are likely to get bored; and players, in the course of trying to maintain an impression of importance, seem to be driven to resort to ever more tortuous techniques. The style of their language, that is, in the search for ascendancy, becomes increasingly literally as well as professedly without meaning.

One consequence of the assertion that there was no authenticity but only contest under the light was the acceptance of the necessity to take sides: how else could there be a game? Propagandists and partisans of all kinds flourished; words became tools not of enquiry but of contention; what mattered was to be part of a team whereby, if there was no truth, then loyalty could take its place. Such commitment without other consideration became more than ever the style of political and social groupings; as if by this, if by nothing else, life might seem worthwhile. Enmity was naturally required to provide the setting for loyalty; the need for belligerence banished any obligation to examine what was being defended or attacked. What a person could be seen to be committed to became the criterion by which he or she, and everything else, might be judged; to take responsibility for oneself on one's own was to put oneself beyond the pale.

And with the need for antagonism, absence of meaning, what can be held up for admiration and entertainment better than spectacular sensationalism in social games? There is argument from time to time about whether the unending flow of murder and torment provided by the entertainment industry inclines those who watch it to perform in such a style themselves: or is the style the effect of how people naturally understand themselves? Nothing can be proved: how on earth in such an area could experiments to test such conjectures be set up? But the facts are there – the style of entertainment on the one hand and the style of commonplace mayhem in the world on the other. And they seem similar enough not to be unconnected. Another common characteristic is one of complaint: when things go wrong, everybody can find satisfaction in blaming everyone else: thus time is consumed, and people need not move from under the arc-lights of the arena. Brains eventually become numbed by such trivial uproar: but then is not this the purpose of grand-guignol or farce? In the meantime however – beneath the blanket of dead wood and fallen leaves in the forest – might not something be moving in the dark?

One possible benefit arising from the vogue for deconstruction might be that by being made aware of the power of prejudices and predilections a person might be given the impetus to look for his or her own – which deconstructionists suggest cannot be done. And indeed it is difficult to see precisely how one might look at the framework through which one has vision – how the eye, as it were, might examine itself. As Wittgenstein put it 'one thinks one is tracing the outline of a thing's nature and one is merely tracing round the frame through which we look at it'. But the point is, that to have a hope of performing such an exercise it would be necessary to move out of the circle of light and go on a journey into the dark – which Wittgenstein in his later writings indeed seemed to recognise. The style would then be one of being alert, sensitive, enquiring and listening; giving attention to what might be one's own prejudices and predilections because in the dark these would obviously be likely to lead one astray. It would be sensed that words, contention, carry the dangers of distraction; but that all these old ghosts might be put to rest with careful attention to what things could be as well as what they are.

It was the philosopher Jon Elster who pointed out that there are certain states which he calls 'essentially by-products': these are 'states that can never be brought about intelligently and intentionally because the attempt to do so precludes the very state that one is attempting to bring about'. That is – such states have to be 'by-products of actions undertaken for other ends' (Jon Elster, *Sour Grapes*). Included in this category are most of those conditions or qualities which might be called 'good': (indeed should not this idea be contained in a definition of what might be called 'good'?). One cannot, for instance, intelligently and intentionally will oneself to be spontaneous, sincere, dignified, authentic: if one tries, one evokes a state the opposite of what has been aimed at. States to do with goodness have to come about not by pursuing them directly but by being attentive to whatever might be required in practical and mundane ways – what is meant by this being recognised perhaps just by the acknowledgement that it is required. One knows, that is, that in pursuit of what might be 'good' one is going on a journey into the dark – with some trust, but no certainty, that one may be guided by, learn from, whatever it is that turns up. No longer battered by the past nor peering uselessly into the future, one might have a chance to make out what is happening in the present – and even if with no certainty, then still with some amusement or excitement. And by such means, as a by-product, one might find that one comes to a view of one's predilections – how odd, looking back, seem one's cavortings under the light! There may be some shame, distress, even fear, at considering these; but also a chance of freedom from the toils of bewilderment and consequent hatred and despair.

There used to be some understanding of this in the Christian idea of 'grace' – that condition which indeed is essentially a by-product; which comes about not of one's own volition though possibly through attentiveness to what might either encourage it or prevent it. What seemed a necessary condition was to begin to have a view of one's own contortions under the light; to see through the beams as it were that were blinding one's eyes. These might for a time have been necessary for protection – there is such bombardment under the light! – and thus such compulsions to justify, to resent, to attack, to defend; to see oneself as heroic and self-sufficient. And such gyrations might even have had to be gone through to make it possible eventually for one to see them as they are. But how else could this be done except from a position in the dark! What might be glimpsed might indeed be some horror at old selves, old ghosts: but without such confrontation, how can any escape be won? But if one takes risks there is always the hope, like that of an artist, that one might come across what one has wondered about but has not known to be there – the experience that if one is attentive, painstaking, then there is in the dark that which works for one; there seem to be fingers other than one's own that lead one to what has been hidden – in paint, in stone, in mind.

'Grace' was defined as a gift of God; but for it to be available one had to accept that it might be there. An impetus was needed to move away from game-playing; a desire to become susceptible to what authenticity might be. None of this need come about as if from a revelation or a thunderbolt from heaven, though there are likely to be frights in the middle of the night – the images of oneself as villain or mountebank or clown. With regard to game-playing one might simply get bored; and just because of this wish to stop. The word 'God' may be useful to describe both the impetus towards change and the realisation of its effects; though there is no need to use words for this at all, and there is always the chance that with too much pinning-down the experience may go. But there are available as it were those fingers out of the dark: the experience of coming into contact with – of being geared into even – a system infinitely larger than oneself. And by means of this, if one has the courage to let it, one may change one's perception of oneself and through this of the world. The understanding is that one is in partnership with the world; which has come about as a result of both everything and nothing to do with one's own efforts.

A journey into the dark is a journey to glimpse what might be the blinkers of one's mind; it is also a journey, by freeing oneself of these, to be able to know what is going on outside. You stretch out your hand: when something seems to take it you may want to turn back; how much easier was life under the arc-lights of enmity and blame! In that hot glow you felt so precisely who and what you were! In the dark there is the danger of the mantrap, the hole; the sudden whiff of gas in the mine. But then – is it not as if you have a bird in your hands? to give notice of, warning of – explosion? of that which will block, that which will expose, a path through the tunnel? Indeed there is danger! But the bird sings so sweetly! Birds are sometimes blinded so that they may sing in the dark. However humans, by the placing of clay on their eyes, have been said to get their sight back. And then if they are no longer, as they once saw themselves, mad archaic figures striding forwards; no longer figures bowed down by the weight of the incomprehensible sky; indeed, what are they? The images move into silence. There may still be validity in the old symbols – the mother and child holding promise of new birth; the man with his arms stretched out as though he were ready to fly; also now indeed, yes, the bird. These may still help to guard one against old horrors, old pathologies. But what one can come to grips with now as if with an art-work are possibilities of sanity – in the outside world; in the mind.

Unpublished, 1998

The Schizoid State

The two main contentions of racism are, firstly, that it is the basis of all human life (Hitler wrote, 'The highest aim of existence is the conservation of the race . . . the maintenance of the racial stock unmixed'); and secondly, that once a man's mind is made up about this, he can never think of changing it. ('All ideas and ideals, all teaching and all knowledge, must serve these ends. It is from this standpoint that everything must be examined and turned to practical use or else discarded'.) Hitler added that he himself had formed his *Weltanschauung* in his early twenties, and since then had 'changed nothing in it'.

A racist is thus a person who not only lives according to what there is reason to think is a fantasy, but who tries to allow no evidence of reason, science, observation or personal experience to touch him.

It is easy to see these characteristics in South Africa today (1960). If you try to reason with an average white South African about race-relations he still assumes you are criticising his country's material care of Africans – the way they are housed and fed. He thus answers you in terms of how much money the government spends on new building, or of his paternal relationship with some loyal office-boy. If you say that this is not what you are talking about – you are talking about votes and freedom of movement and trade unions – then a blank look comes over his face and he has nothing to answer you. This is not because your argument has stumped him but because he finds you unintelligible. To him it is as if you were talking about horses. You cannot reasonably discuss whether horses should be given the franchise. It is a situation that has silenced philosophers – the man who looks at a human being and says that *he* calls it something else.

The racist also won't accept the universal evidence of anthropologists, biologists and sociologists that his racial classifications are nonsense. He prefers his own imaginative analogies drawn usually from bull-breeding. (Hitler had a variation – 'The titmouse cohabits only with the titmouse, the fieldmouse with the fieldmouse, the housemouse with the housemouse'.) He won't have looked at the work of scientists who say that racial classifications are not only illusory but even destructive of the evolution they are supposed to promote; that evolution depends on the opportunity for varieties to mingle; that the decision to treat men as animals does in fact reduce, as under Hitler, those who practise this to the level of animals. The convictions of a racist are stronger than evidence or science.

The disease of racism in an individual, psychologists say, arises from the refusal to face the evil or 'dark' side of oneself, and a transference of it on to some group that appears different, in order that one may continue to think of oneself as elect and sinless. This refusal is made when facts arise in one's experience which are painful and frightening to bear. These are natural and inevitable occurrences; but if such facts are faced, then by the very undergoing of this ordeal, there is growth both in knowledge and in further capacity for courage and understanding. This is how spiritual growth happens. But if painful facts about oneself are not faced, then there is a blockage in the path of normal growth and a deviation towards some dead-end of personality.

The normal growth of human societies, scientists say, depends upon the acceptance of ever greater complexities and comprehensiveness. If a society refuses these, it deviates up some dead branch of evolution.

Nature has its own savage remedies. Racism involves violence, and there may be a cure to it in violence. Most Germans have now been cured of Hitlerism; they were cured by slaughter, savagery and hopelessness. There came a time when reality could be evaded no longer, and the survivors faced it. But millions were dead.

In South Africa it is obvious to most people that sooner or later the white Afrikaners will lose and the non-racists will win. This will happen in the course of history. But the question of practical importance is whether this process has to be undergone in huge misery and slaughter, or whether it can be transposed to the level of painstakingly looking at evidence and enduring and learning.

Spectator, 1960

The Burden of Vocation

Anti-Semitism – The Longest Hatred. By Robert S. Wistrich

In his introduction Professor Wistrich says that it is not the job of
a historian to 'give any definite reply' to questions concerning 'why'
there is anti-Semitism. What a historian can do is to 'illuminate the
mechanisms and consequences of anti-Semitism in different social,
cultural and political contexts'. This Professor Wistrich proceeds to
do clearly and well. In addition to the comparatively well-known
horror stories of medieval and modern European anti-Semitism, here
are accounts of such pathology in the Hellenistic and Roman worlds,
also of how the plague has taken root in the contemporary Arab world
– as part of the hostility to Israel, but containing much of the squalid
demonology of traditional Western anti-Semitism.

But the very clarity of exposition leaves a reader with an urgent need
to look at the question 'why'. Without such an attempt the chronicle
takes on the aura of something decreed by fate – which presumably is
what anti-Semites wish to hear.

Professor Wistrich recognises that there are two focal points in the
histories he is presenting. At the centre of anti-Semitism there is an
obsessive fear about a Jewish conspiracy to dominate the world: and
at the centre of Judaism there is, in spite of secularisation, the 'pride'
of Jews 'in their special vocation as a people covenanted by God'. It
is difficult not to notice a connection here. But Professor Wistrich
prefers to hang on to the by now largely accepted notion that Jews
are unwitting scapegoats for gentile inadequacy and fear.

In this context there is mentioned an interesting gloss – the idea
that it may have been the confusions of simple-minded Christians
when faced with the subtleties and paradoxes of their own religion that
caused them, for instance, to instigate the calumny that Jews require
Christian blood in order to bake their Passover bread: this may have
arisen from befuddled Christian guilt about the drinking the blood of

their own God. This would fit in with the Gnostic idea that Christianity is too sophisticated a religion for the simple-minded – a belief that would seem to be borne out by Christians *en masse* throughout the ages. But about any connection between the focal points in these histories, and the question 'why', Professor Wistrich is largely silent.

It seems to me that at the back of anti-Semitism is the conspiracy theory of history – the conviction that human affairs proceed not in accordance with chance or with patterns set up by oneself and other persons such as oneself, but through the agency of stronger and mainly malignant powers that one has to guard against and fight if one is not to be destroyed. This is a simple-minded view of affairs for which there is no evidence, and concerning which efforts can surely be made to show that it is pathological.

However at the back of the question why primitive-minded gentiles choose to unload their pathologies on to Jews it is not improper, surely, to see the very strength and tenacity of the special way in which Jews see themselves as qualities that so tragically make this possible. And the question can surely be asked – Granted that Jews do not see themselves as 'chosen' for anything so phantasmagorical and absurd as world domination, what on earth do they see themselves as chosen, covenanted by God in a special vocation, *for?*

One of the peculiarities and indeed perils of contemporary discourse about anti-Semitism is that even a question such as this can be taken as anti-Semitic; and it is because of this that there is so little decent approach to the question 'why'. Professor Wistrich tells with approval a story of how General de Gaulle, having once remarked that the Jews were 'an elite people, sure of itself and domineering', was taken to task by the critic Raymond Aron for having thus 'knowingly, voluntarily, opened a new era in Jewish history and perhaps in the history of anti-Semitism'. But what sense is there in umbrage being taken by a people at being called a sure-of-itself elite? Perhaps it is the accusation of being 'domineering' that makes alarm bells ring. But fear of this is surely a facet of pathology.

Jews have, against all odds, maintained a sense of identity and vocation. This vocation was at first to occupy a piece of land; then, according to the Torah, to be that in which 'shall all families of the earth be blessed'. For many centuries Jews, while keeping their sense of a calling, seemed to have lost this latter sense of what they were being called for. Now that they have re-established the first part of their vocation regarding land, might they not look more to the second, regarding some responsibility for at least their neighbours? There have been intimations from their prophets that they might at times have been called to carry this out.

Christians have tried to take upon themselves the second part of this calling. But then they for the most part do not seem to have been given much of the subtlety of mind required for the job.

Sunday Telegraph, 1991

Self-Deceit and Lack of Courage

The Architect of Genocide – Himmler and the Final Solution.
By Richard Breitman

For the most part this book is a re-hash of the familiar sickening story of events that led up to the Holocaust. The role of Himmler is stressed but hardly explained; there is little attempt to portray his history or his personality. Any virtue that resides in a reader being reminded of such horrors is soon outweighed by the impression that without an effort to understand the human drives at the back of them they become almost meaningless: what might seem to be a salutary message becomes obscured by the buzz of scholarship. It is as if one were reading of atrocities performed by robots. There is thus little help in the business of trying to see how such events might not happen again.

If one makes one's own efforts to dig about in this book one can learn that Himmler was someone obsessed with the idea of imposing order on what might seem chaos: he thought it was the role of humans to achieve such order 'cleanly' and 'neatly'. This involved purifying the human species from abnormalities that might be perpetuated genetically: to Himmler 'normality' meant a strain of pure 'Nordic blood'. The first step towards a 'final solution' to this problem was taken soon after the Nazis came to power; a policy of euthanasia was implemented to kill lunatics and those with physical deformities. From this, given the Nazi ideology, it was only a further step to the idea that all those who deviated from the fantasy-ideal of 'Nordic blood' were genetically harmful. Thus along with the mentally ill and physically handicapped there were soon lumped gypsies, Slavs, Poles and above all Jews. The latter were the largest and, to Nazi eyes, most dangerous sub-group in their midst, since they were so clearly – all honour to them – differentiated from the Nazi ideal.

To Himmler, given the premise of the necessity of racial purity, it seemed 'logical' and 'scientific' to get rid of Jews. For a time in the '30s the talk was not of extermination, although the idea had been just round the corner since the time of Hitler's *Mein Kampf*, but rather of resettlement. The difficult question was – where? The favourite suggested destination was Madagascar: it was calculated that 'with 120 ships carrying an average of fifteen hundred Jews in each the process would take about four years'. But the practical difficulties of implementing such a plan struck even such fantasts as leading Nazis. Hitler conceded that such an operation might be feasible only if there was a war. It seems sometimes that idealists such as Himmler and Hitler desired war mainly as a means of implementing their racialist programme. Certainly, when the war was under way the priorities given to the activities of the death squads hindered the German war effort.

Before this time it had become evident that logistics made it impracticable to give any geographical answer to the question 'where' concerning resettlement: if Nazi ideology was to be implemented, Jews would have to be killed. There remained the question of how this might be done 'cleanly' and 'neatly' – in physical and also in mental terms. After the Kristallnacht of 1938 in which atrocities had been performed openly against Jews, it was said that Himmler had had to go into a sanatorium – he was distressed not about the fact of the atrocities, but about their having been performed so publicly and messily.

In the early years of the war Jews, along with Poles and Slavs, were killed in trenches in which they were made to lie and then were machine-gunned. But this, it was noted, had a debilitating effect on those who had to do the shooting. It was thus that the concept and practicability of gas chambers were laboriously worked out. A pretence could be made that what were being constructed and organised were 'de-lousing chambers' or 'baths': and thus the susceptibilities of SS soldiers might be spared – also those of the innumerable bureaucrats who got the gigantic operation under way.

So what lessons might after all be learned from this grim business? First, it can be stressed that the concept of 'purity of blood' is in no way scientific; that it is in fact the opposite of scientific to imagine that the human species might be improved by genetic manipulation or selective breeding. By these it is true that one might produce a strain of humans with, for instance, some larger limb or increased bone-headedness, but scientists understand that any lively step forwards in evolution depends on the free interplay between environment and chance – this alone ensuring that what will be selected will in any real sense be 'fittest'.

Secondly there can be observed the style of mind of a person who is convinced that he is more fitted to survive than, for instance, Slavs and Poles and Jews. Himmler wrote –

> Here stands a world as we have conceived it: beautiful decent, socially equal . . . a happy, beautiful world full of culture; this is what our Germany is like. On the other side stands a population of 180 million, a mixture of races, whose very names are unpronounceable and whose physique is such that one can shoot them without pity or compassion.

What seemed to be lacking in Himmler and Hitler and those like them is any capacity to look at themselves, and at what is in fact going on around them. Such people are incapable of seeing any impurity in themselves – they are too frightened of it to see it – and so they project it on to others, where they are frightened of it too but these others can be wiped out. The whole process is justified by what is supposed to be logic; but in fact it depends on self-deceit and a lack of courage. Even well-drilled SS soldiers were revolted by the effects of such policies when they were out in the open, not hidden. It takes a massive system of falsehood to obliterate such common human reactions; and it is by ensuring that a system does not overcome an individual's innate capacity for responsibility that such events might not happen again.

Daily Telegraph, 1991

Becoming Free of the Burden

The Sacred Executioner: Human Sacrifice and the Legacy of Guilt.
By Hyam Maccoby

It is the contention of this book that human sacrifice is 'particularly connected historically with the foundation of a new human grouping, whether a tribe, a city or a religion'. Judaism was founded on the near-sacrifice of Isaac by Abraham; Christianity was founded on the sacrifice of Christ. There seems to be a demand for sacrifice at such moments of change because transformation only takes place at the cost of some destruction. By ritualising destruction in sacrifice, humans can try to render it harmless and absolve themselves from guilt. The demand is thus for scapegoats on whom destructiveness can be blamed; then the true perpetrators can move forward to new life as if innocent. The scapegoats are seen as 'sacred executioners' who are both accursed because of their imagined deed and yet sacred because those who cast them in the role know at some level that the deed has been necessary. The archetype for all this is Cain; on whose forehead, after the murder of Abel, there was placed a mark that signified both his being outcast and his being given God's protection.

Mr Maccoby concentrates on the difference between the Jewish idea of sacrifice in which an original impulse to make an offering of humans to God is transferred to the sacrifice of animals and to rituals such as circumcision; and the Christian idea of sacrifice, in which the victim is the human God and the role of scapegoat (in Mr Maccoby's view) is taken on by Jews. Mr Maccoby's theme is that for the Jews God himself was in some way the Sacred Executioner: the business of the bearing of guilt was contained within the Jews' peculiar mythology concerning their relationship with their own God. Christians however seemed to need a scapegoat outside the area of their destructiveness, and Jews were chosen for this because, historically, they could both be blamed for Christ's death and yet in some sense be seen as sacred because of their kinship with him. Also indeed it is part of Christian mythology that without Christ's execution there would be no atonement for the sins of the world. Thus for centuries Jews have been horribly persecuted by Christians and yet, Mr Maccoby claims, Christians have preserved a sense of Jews' usefulness. It was a post-Christian generation exemplified by the Nazis who believed in their own perfectibility and thus did not feel the need for the recipients of any guilt, who stopped sensing the usefulness of those who were amongst them and yet apart from them, and so set about wiping them out.

Early parts of Mr Maccoby's book are concerned with comparisons between Israelite and Kenite mythologies in order to establish his case: these will be of more interest to scholars than to laymen. It is when Mr Maccoby gets into his stride of explaining the mechanisms of what has so often been the loathsome behaviour of so-called Christians to Jews that his book becomes of potent interest. With the rise of the cult of the Virgin Mary in the eleventh century, for instance, there was the concomitant idea that it was the body and blood of the Infant Jesus that was eaten and drunk at the Mass; and it was because of this, Mr Maccoby suggests, that stories arose of Jews murdering and drinking the blood of infant Christians – as a projection of Christian feelings of guilt.

There are always vicious impulses such as those of anti-Semitism lurking in minds' alleyways: it is salutary to have descriptions of them reiterated and explained. But this area has, since the events of the 1930s and 1940s, been fairly well looked at; and Christians sometimes allow themselves to be sitting targets for the receiving back of their own guilt. Mr Maccoby suggests that Christians have always placed total blame for the crucifixion on Jews and have dismissed the part played, for instance, by the Romans. But it seems to me that this is an error that has become part of Jewish as well as of anti-Semitic mythology. In the Christian creed it is Pontius Pilate and not Caiaphas who is specifically mentioned as being in charge of the crucifixion, and in the mainstream of Christian theology it has always been held that both Pilate and the Jewish crowd that called for Jesus' execution are representative of the whole of humanity – of you and me.

A book that can profitably be read in conjunction with *The Sacred Executioner* is Dan Jacobson's recent *The Story of the Stories*. This looks at a way in which Jews might see themselves and be seen – as humans, as they grow up, have usually to be seen – as responsible for themselves. It looks at the extraordinary predicaments in which Jews have placed both themselves and the people round them by their paradoxical mythology. Jews believe that they are the chosen people of a God that is especially theirs and yet also through them of the whole world. When God wishes to punish the Jews for disobedi-ence he uses the Assyrians, for instance, to effect this punishment; when he wants to show his love again for his people he punishes the Assyrians for having obeyed his instructions. With such a capricious and all-powerful 'executioner' God, it has been difficult for Jews to see exactly where their own responsibilities lie. It has been easy for them to see themselves, as well as for others to see them, in the role of scapegoats.

In the days of the Old Testament, Jews, along with the rest of humanity, felt justified in the periodic slaughter of their neighbours: then for nearly two thousand years they maintained some moral integrity regarding the avoidance of aggressive violence by being in a position in which they did not have the burden of wielding power. This was some growing-up in the sense that there were fewer chances for projection and exculpation; but now in Israel again, Jews like most other nations have in some sense to become executioners in order to survive. The problem for modern humanity seems to be whether or not it learns how to handle the problems involving the destructiveness attendant on the business of wielding power without either the need to project guilt or the tendency to throw away all moral concepts: either humanity learns this, or it seems likely to blow itself up. Jews have hitherto indeed seemed specially equipped to see many of humanity's paradoxes: the world now seems to be watching them, after their years in the wilderness, to see whether or not they may have learned how consciously to handle the creative/destructive nature of the exercise of power. To have too high expectations of this difficult endeavour might be thought to be placing another burden upon Jews; but then it was they who told in the first place of the lively purposefulness of their burden-placing God.

Listener, 1983

Are Not Humans Responsible for Themselves?

Bruno Bettelheim: the Other Side of Madness. By Nina Sutton

Bruno Bettelheim was a concentration-camp survivor who said that he had learned much from the experience. He later ran a school for autistic children in America, and claimed that with care and skill they could be cured. He was seen as something of a saint in his heyday of the 1960s; after his suicide in 1990 he was for a time reviled as an anachronism and a fraud.

Bettelheim was born into a bourgeois Jewish family in Vienna in 1903. As a young man he ran the family lumber business until the Nazis took it over. He then spent a year in Dachau and Buchenwald before obtaining his release and emigrating to America in 1939. In Chicago he established himself as a psychoanalyst and became head of the Orthogenic School for seriously disturbed children; he achieved world fame through his writings both on his concentration camp experiences and on how to deal with so-called madness. Controversy arose from his propositions that suffering and evil could be made use of if one learned to look, with part of oneself, on the rest of oneself as an object to which things happened that had meaning; also that psychotic children could be helped by something of the same approach. His detractors claimed that although his attitudes about learning from evil might have relevance to pre-war Dachau and Buchenwald, it was outrageous to suppose they might be appropriate to extermination camps such as Auschwitz. He was also accused of exaggerating the stories and incidence of success with learning at his school, and of having on occasions performed unacceptable acts of violence on his children.

This book tells a vastly complex story which demands finely balanced assessments; these Nina Sutton, an Anglo-French journalist, achieves successfully.

The most publicly passionate controversy that Bettelheim became involved in was occasioned by the Eichmann trial in 1961. Bettelheim joined Hannah Arendt and others in suggesting that Jews, because of their tradition of fatalism and what was called 'ghetto thinking' should accept some responsibility for what happened to them at the time of the Holocaust; it was only by this that any repetition could be prevented. Those who wished to deny this could, and did, call such an attitude anti-Semitic.

In his school it was Bettelheim's aim to get the children to think for themselves and thus to find meaning: it was because to them the world made no sense that they resorted to senseless acts of violence and self-destruction. When he was asked about his acts of anger and slapping against a child, he replied: 'I much prefer that he should hate me than himself'. Bettelheim felt that it was often the unconscious hostility of a parent, usually the mother, which resulted in self-blame and self-hatred in a child; and that these could be alleviated by being brought into the open and accepted. Regarding those ex-pupils who told stories of his eccentric behaviour, it was evident that they who had once been designated psychotic were now strikingly self-possessed and lucid – so there had been in fact some curing.

Towards the end of his life Bettelheim relinquished his school and it seemed that he could no longer find meaning: perhaps at Auschwitz humanity had come to a dead end after all. His wife, on whom he had depended, died; he tried without success to settle with his children. At the age of eighty-six, in an old people's home which he hated, and after a series of incapacitating illnesses, he decided that if there was no more meaning in life, then there might be in death; so he took some barbiturates, had a drink, put a plastic bag over his head, and died. Some of his ex-pupils said that they felt let down.

What this book is uncommonly good at is giving the sense of vital and global conundrums being faced without the compulsion to offer simplistic judgements. Bettelheim, a largely self-trained analyst, complained that Freud and his followers recognised the unconscious and tried to ease it toward consciousness, but then underestimated the power and complexity of what remained. He himself, by striving to uncover or to construct 'meaning', managed to lead an immensely fruitful life; at the end, however, there would always be death.

In the meantime there would be confrontation with the baffling realities by which humans can learn to think and act and be responsible for themselves.

Daily Telegraph, 1995

Some Do Take Responsibility for Themselves

White or Black: Images of Africa and Blacks in Western Popular Culture.
By Jan Nederveen Pieterse

This is a coffee-table type of book written in a scholarly style on the subject of the images that white people have of blacks in Western popular culture. Its assumptions are, first, the fashionable academic one that 'there are no facts, only interpretations'; and following from this, that blacks cannot help accepting the interpretations put upon them by dominant whites – that any change in 'racism' will depend exclusively on a change in the attitudes of whites.

One of the shortcomings of this approach is that it does not distinguish between what might be deep in human nature (a 'fact') and what might be excrescences of certain human societies. Pieterse recognises that people tend naturally to look on things in categories; to notice differences between 'us' and 'them'. But from this he seems to suggest that there is something wrong in human cognition; that properly everything should be seen as much the same as everything else. This does indeed seem to be an interpretation and not a fact.

In fact, the numerous illustrations that Pieterse gives, both in pictures and in text, of white attitudes to blacks over the years – in storybooks, in advertising, in films – give quite a kindly if condescending image of blacks: blacks appear as children, entertainers, loyal servants, clowns: Little Black Sambo, Uncle Tom, Jim Crow. Even the frequent cartoons depicting, for instance, cannibalism, show smiling 'natives' stoking fires under cooking pots in which missionaries seem to be being given the chance to make witty remarks. There is almost nothing of the disgusting virulence that has been the hallmark over the years of cartoons and propaganda extolling anti-Semitism. And after the Civil Rights Movement of the 1960s even the more condescending images about blacks changed – golliwogs were banned, Mary Poppins and Dr Doolittle censored – so that this was, indeed, an acceptance by whites of some responsibility for their imagery.

But there is something dangerous about this insistence on the exclusive responsibility of whites. To take from blacks any responsibility for their own predicament is an ultimate form of paternalism or 'colonialism': it is insisting that, in order to assuage white guilt, only whites shall have the privilege of human freedom of action and choice. This was the attitude so strongly fought against by Steve Biko and his Black Consciousness Movement in South Africa: Biko saw that there is no virtue for blacks in just blaming whites for their predicament, even in accepting help by way of the whites guiltily blaming themselves; what was required was for blacks to take on the business of altering their perceptions of themselves, and to be proud enough to believe that this might alter other people's perceptions of them – and thus their predicament. This would involve confrontations; but the successful outcome of these would depend on the self-confidence of blacks.

Pieterse's book is confusing because although he does seem to see how images of blacks in popular culture are in fact changing due to the efforts and achievements of admired blacks, for most of its length the book seems to have to make obeisance, itself slave-like, to current obsessions concerning 'racism', 'classism', 'sexism' (the 'Big Three' as Pieterse calls them), in which sense and evidence have to be denied for the sake of current jargon and current battles. Perhaps it may be blacks themselves, with their special aptitude for laughter and debunking (what an unfashionable idea!) who will put an end to the daft notion that everyone is the same as everyone else; who will be proud enough of their own special attributes to tell whites (or women, or the intelligentsia, or whomever) that they should be proud of theirs – and thus get on with the business of appreciating both themselves and one another and working in harmony.

Somewhere deep in this book is the glimpse that the white intellectual's frenzied insistence on taking refuge behind 'isms' is a symptom of the intellectual himself having lost his sense of identity and function; of his seeking safety as a slave. Perhaps soon a black scholar will give us a book on the ghastly self-lacerating images that whites currently put upon themselves in films, in soap-operas, in novels. But then it is to be hoped that a black intellectual will not feel guilty about any part he might unwittingly have played in giving to whites such guilt; but will tell them just – For God's sake, get on with sorting out yourselves.

Daily Telegraph, 1992

Jonestown Enigmas

Black and White. By Shiva Naipaul

The first half of this book is an account of the author's experience as an investigator into the Jonestown massacre in 1978, in which more than 900 followers of the Reverend Jim Jones killed themselves by drinking cyanide in their commune in Guyana. Shiva Naipaul does not retell the story in detail; he trusts his readers to remember something of the factual accounts at the time. What he is interested in are the story's ramifications and implications. He seems to suggest that these are so paradoxical that they can only properly be described in terms that are enigmatic. He does not try to put his insights into the black and white terms of his title. To do so might be to fall into some trap symptomatic of the disaster that is being described.

Jim Jones's People's Temple Brotherhood began in Indiana, flourished in San Francisco, ended in the forests of Guyana. It was a community of the poor, the dropouts, the ex-junkies, mostly black, for whom established society had no place. Under the leadership of Jim Jones they found a sense of belonging: of something to live for. Jim Jones's success was witnessed by eminent visitors. Even in Guyana, in conditions of hardship and some brutality, his followers wrote of their happiness and feelings of fulfilment. But others wrote of the violence of the commune – its sickness and despair. One of the paradoxes that Shiva Naipaul had to face from the beginning was the existence, side by side, of accounts of ecstasy and horror.

Jones, when young, had been described as 'a Hitler'; he himself admired Stalin. The stories that came back from the commune were like those that came out of Germany or Russia in the 1930s – of either heaven or hell. There seemed to be no language to make sense of these from a higher viewpoint – either among people involved in the experience, or among those describing it.

Jim Jones felt his commune threatened: there was a group who called themselves Concerned Relatives trying to free from the commune children whom they claimed were held there by force; there was a U.S. congressman coming on a fact-finding mission. Jones had been issuing warnings to his disciples that as a last resort against persecution they might have to prove their loyalty to him and their ideals by a suicide pact: they even went through the motions of practising this. The impressions of being beleaguered were largely imaginary or self-induced: but they seemed to be necessary to the sense of belonging – of being ready to suffer pain and even death for the pleasure of having something to live for.

Shiva Naipaul runs his observant eye over the conditions that perhaps have always been required for the cohesion of societies – the feeling that there are enemies without and possibly traitors within; the readiness of members to die for the sake of what gives their life meaning. The second half of the book is a rather haphazard rumination on the history of protest-movements and utopia-movements in California in the '60s and '70s. In these much of what had begun as fierce if narrow-minded drives to social betterment ended in a cynical acceptance that the conventional status quo could not be beaten – even if this led to self-destruction. Shiva Naipaul describes these cavortings with a wry horror; as if he were looking down on an ants' nest. He sees his job as describing the ants' nest, not explaining it; let alone (as Marx might have noted) changing it.

The basic paradox faced here is that most human beings do not like to feel alone, they like to give their devotion to a person or to a society, and it is easier to maintain these bonds if one feels oneself threatened. And so unless there are sophisticated safeguards as it were built into such persons or societies, pressures will build up in them either to launch an attack on the real or imagined enemy or, if they are not strong enough for this, to involve themselves in some loyal self-immolation. And all this is done, of course, within an aura of joy and love. Shiva Naipaul quotes Che Guevara: 'A revolutionary death is the reality: victory is the dream'. He quotes a father whose daughters died at Jonestown: 'We will all, one of these days, be forced to drink nuclear suicide'. There seems to be a satisfaction in such statements: people will die at least huddled together.

But this book lacks some recognition for all its cleverness and courage – and it must have been hard to keep going, let alone stay sane, on the edge of such a charnel house. But it is the fact that Shiva Naipaul was able to do just this gives some hope beyond the self-destructiveness of humans and of societies who see things in projected blacks and whites. Yet it is this sense that is missing from the book. Very occasionally there is a glimpse of Shiva Naipaul himself from the outside, trudging round San Francisco collecting information hand-in-hand with his five-year-old son. This is a view of someone almost but not quite solitarily going about in a society he is horrified by and which he cannot wholly escape from; but he is looking down on it coolly, and he knows there are others doing the same; and it is a reader's awareness of this that gives hope. We are all in a society which, with its stockpiles of bombs, seems no less than others to be ready to defend itself by self-destruction. But by carrying this thought in mind it is perhaps as if one were in the company of a child that might survive.

Listener, 1980

Evil Is Done by Ordinary People Going about Their Ordinary Tasks

Paris and the Third Reich: A History of the German Occupation, 1940-1944. By David Pryce-Jones

This book is in the coffee-table format of text-with-pictures. At first it gives the impression of being rather a *Harper's Bazaar* view of the German occupation of Paris. The text is littered with the names of 'top' people in the way that they crop up in the gossip columns of magazines: these seem, as usual, almost too irrelevant to be true. But then the impression grows that this might be a valid way of writing about the social aspects of Nazism. It is as if the attractions and even the powers of Nazism did perhaps reside in its providing some sort of political glamour by which people who care about such things could be fashionably bedazzled.

After the first shock of the defeat in 1940, there was a certain euphoria in Paris: a Frenchwoman, watching German troops march in, called out 'Will you just look at those lovely men!' A popular magazine described German soldiers as 'decent, helpful, above all correct'. There was almost no hatred. For people who had money life went on as usual: in restaurants steaks were still 'grilled to perfection'; brothel owners had 'never been so happy'; even the arts flourished – collaboration, it was said, meant 'Mozart in Paris'. Soon there were more books being published in France than in America; more films being made than in Germany.

To be a collaborator at first was simply normal: 'People did not think of themselves as having moral choices to make, they had careers and ambitions instead'. Inevitably in these circumstances it was the doings of 'top' people that were noted and remembered. But without the willing cooperation of an enormous number of ordinary French people it would have been impossible for the Germans to run the occupied zone. The French police force outnumbered the entire German garrison, yet they obeyed the Germans: they had, after all, been taught obedience. Half a million French workers were paid above average wages to build fortifications and naval bases along the coast: they had, after all, accepted the idea that what mattered was high wages.

Even in areas in which people had become accustomed to ask questions there was a change perhaps of content but not of style. 'Collaborationists versus non-collaborationists was the latest of the many politico-literary realignments which have proverbially made Paris salons and cafés so enthrallingly contentious'. The question of who might one day be shot, and by whom, became something of a party game.

As the war went on there was the hideous matter of the deportation of Jews; and later the question of who had, or who had not, chosen to notice this. But such questions were confused by the Germans' skill at exploiting the Jewish community's own instinct that 'safety lay in obeying the law', so that orders about assembly could be issued through the Jewish leaders themselves. Thus it was that Jews 'did not turn to resistance, with unforeseeable consequences'. Over 75,000 Jews were deported from France: some 3,000 survived.

During the period of the Hitler-Stalin pact, Communists were even more keen than others to do the conventional thing by becoming Fascist: they were certainly used to obedience, and to be ready to sacrifice themselves for a cause. After the German attack on Russia in 1941, they obediently set about becoming active in resistance; but here once more they were true to type – 'energies which might have been turned against the German troops were dissipated in factionalism'. It was only late in 1943 that the 'huge passive majority' felt itself 'in a position to decide safely on which side it would be preferable to finish'.

About 1,800 French hostages were executed by the Germans: after the liberation perhaps 30-40,000 collaborators were executed by Frenchmen. 'What the French did to themselves after the occupation was in some ways more painful than what the Germans had done to them during it'. The evils resultant on turning a blind eye affected oneself, eventually, as much as others.

This melancholy story has been well researched by David Pryce-Jones; it is chronicled lucidly in a compendium-of-anecdotes style. The blurb announces: 'He does not seek to pass judgements but rather to establish the facts'. This book will provide a valuable service if it reaches the wide audience at which it is aimed. But there is still the question of whether this fact-presenting service will not be somewhat vitiated by the lack of attempt at judgement about matters that at first sight seem paradoxical.

What emerges from the story is an illustration of what Hannah Arendt has called 'the banality of evil' – the way in which with just a switch as it were of custom, evil is done by ordinary people going about their ordinary tasks. It is the acceptance of whatever happens to be taken for granted that does the damage: it is through loyal people, respectable people, that evil projects succeed. Over and over again after the liberation there were excuses – we were only obeying orders; we were only doing our duty by our country, our government, our laws. Even conventional law-breakers, as it were, prospered under the Nazis: the Nazi hierarchy got their supplies and their loot through rackets run by French gangsters. Within the Nazi organisation there seemed to be a role for every organisation-man: the only people who were excluded were those who naturally had interests other than, and even a contempt for, the normal workings of 'society', and even for self-advancement. Concerning these, the switch in custom that seems to have taken place was just that society now accepted that such outsiders had no real right to live. And without them the lump was left without the leaven.

Two German characters awaken sympathy in this book: one is Ernst Jünger, the novelist, who wandered through Paris during these days somewhat agonised and helpless but with a discerning and compassionate eye: and the other is Heinrich von Stülpnagel, the Military Governor of Paris, who became implicated in the bomb-plot against Hitler, and when it failed tried to commit suicide but was resuscitated and tortured and hanged. Against the former there can be the criticism that he was a passive observer of evil: against the latter there could be the charge that he actively betrayed the commission that he still ostensibly honoured. But both men would have known that in circumstances in which evil is banal there are no simple moral choices: there are only choices between evils. If one wishes to remain sane what is unequivocal is the need for perception and discernment; what happens then is often decided for one. The easiest attitude, of course, is to allow oneself to become blind: this is the unequivocal evil.

Listener, 1981

Cold Feet

The Tragedy of Leon Trotsky. By Ronald Segal

There are questions of enduring interest that remain about Trotsky. Why did not he, instead of Stalin, come to power after Lenin's death in 1924; and if he had, how different would have been the history of Russia and of the world? Was there something in his nature, and is there something in the nature of power, that makes it difficult to imagine Trotsky taking on that kind of responsibility? Isaac Deutscher's massive biography, written during the 1950s and '60s, however authoritative, was too scholarly and too much in the Marxist tradition to give emphasis to such hypothetical questions. Mr Segal puts them in the forefront of his book, and they perhaps explain why Trotsky is still such a controversial figure today in the worlds both of fringe politics and of political theory.

Trotsky had been more dramatically at the centre of the Russian Revolution even than Lenin: he had organised street-fighting, roused factory workers, led troops, while Lenin still waited in the wings disguised in a red wig. Trotsky was then put in charge of the armed forces which defeated the counterrevolution. In 1917 Lenin himself proposed that Trotsky should be made Chairman of the Soviet of People's Commissars – virtually head of government. Trotsky had reason to decline this offer, which had been a tactical move on the part of Lenin who was the obvious natural leader. But from that moment until Lenin's death Trotsky was the obvious and natural heir-apparent.

Mr Segal states that it is quite clear that the reason Trotsky did not get power in 1924 was simply that he did not want it: whenever power was offered to him, or was within his grasp, he simply turned away, whatever were his later explanations and justifications. During 1923, when Lenin lay dying and the rest of the Party élite were intriguing about the succession, Trotsky remained aloof; when his aloofness seemed to be in itself some sort of decision, he became ill; his illness was recognised by his doctors to be 'mysterious'. (It started when he was out duck-shooting and, literally, got cold feet.) This illness recurred at moments of crisis during the next few years while Stalin manipulated the bureaucratic machinery to suit his own ends. Then, when there was no longer any chance of his getting power, Trotsky's illness left him, and he threw himself wholeheartedly into the business of opposition.

Mr Segal is wary of the suggestion that the illness was psychosomatic: he is more bold in suggesting the nature of the conflict in reasoning that might have caused it. Before the Revolution, Trotsky had broken with Lenin because he had seen that Lenin's insistence on ruthless party discipline would 'lead in the end only to the degradation of despotism'. But then he had realised that 'it was Lenin's way alone in the end that had led towards the socialist revolution'. So, when the battle came, he rejoined Lenin, and occasionally himself descended to 'degradations of despotism' – ruthlessly ordering the death of revolutionaries who were demanding the democratic rights promised by the revolution. But when the battle was over he saw the danger of despotism again. And so, Mr Segal says, there was a chasm which Trotsky 'would never manage to close' between the realisation, on the one hand, that the revolution could not be maintained without despotism, and the knowledge, on the other, that despotism was just what the revolution had been designed to destroy.

Stalin, of course, did away with the gap simply by staking everything on such despotism that not only were revolutionaries who happened to disagree with him killed, but so was almost everyone who could be called a revolutionary – since every revolutionary might have a memory of the promise to end despotism. On the theoretical level, the battle was between Stalin's insistence that socialism should be consolidated in just one country, Russia, which Marx had said was impossible, and Trotsky's belief that socialism was only possible if there was world revolution, which Marx had said should inevitably be happening but wasn't. This gave Trotsky the opportunity for endless rhetoric. The conflict went on in a fog of words – Marx's theories were tailored to fit apparent facts, facts were tailored to fit apparent theories – but what was happening, in effect, was that the protagonists were separating towards the two poles of the insoluble dilemma: Stalin was going for power without morality, and Trotsky was being driven into the powerless moralising of permanent opposition.

Mr Segal emphasises the intellectual repugnance that Trotsky felt towards Stalin: Stalin was a mediocrity; Stalinism was merely the

exercise of the brutal and the banal. Trotsky was interested in literature and the arts; he himself wrote two or three good books; he was
at home in discussions of morals and aesthetics. But Mr Segal does
not make enough of Trotsky's almost physical recoil not only from the
brutality of the new leaders but from the social tedium associated with
them – and with almost all exercises of power. In his autobiography
Trotsky says of Stalin's élite (in a passage not quoted by Mr Segal):
'If I took no part in the amusements which were becoming more and
more common in the lives of the new governing stratum, it was not
for moral reasons, but because I hated to inflict such boredom on
myself. The visiting at each others' homes, the assiduous attendance
at the ballet, the drinking parties at which people who were absent
were pulled to pieces, had no attraction for me.' He might well have
said the same sort of thing about political life in, say, Washington
or London. Trotsky's repugnance was not simply, as he imagined,
for Stalinism: it was for what seem to be habitual conditions for the
enjoyment of power.

Trotsky could never understand how such mediocre people could
keep a hold on power: he believed a sensible proletariat must rise up
and smash them. But in this, as Mr Segal says, he was simply 'innocent'.
As a good Marxist he looked at history, but always through the rosy
spectacles of faith in the coming rule of the proletariat. If he had seen
history straight, then 'history might have shown him the paradox by
which triviality of thought has informed an immensity of violence,
and vanity has manifested itself in the fullness of evil'. It was Stalin
who went on to be for a time one of the most successful politicians in
history – successful in that he managed to achieve almost everything
he had aimed at – a monolithic, bureaucratic tyranny exercised over
a large part of Europe and Asia. And this was not in spite of squalid
mediocrity, but because of it. And it was Trotsky, the man of reason
and sensibility, who could not see the banal nature of evil, and so did
not see how it might be prevented, and so was banished and killed.

At moments, he seemed to see politics as something like the
creation of a work of art; out of which, after struggle, something
beautiful should emerge. He also imagined that it might be just
the continuing struggle that would be beautiful. This latter idea
was indeed more like that of an artist than a Marxist. For much of
his life he did seem to manage to stay on the tightrope above the
chasm of purely denunciatory prophecy on the one hand, and the
arrogance of power on the other; he managed this too in his books
My Life and *The History of the Russian Revolution*, both of which had
qualities as art. For the rest, in his justifications and his polemics,

he too often fell into one or other of the two abysses. He found it impossible publicly to reconcile himself to the idea that it might be in'the nature of things that 'Stalins' would be the sort of people who held power; that 'Trotskys' might sometimes lead romantic wars, but were the sort of people who afterwards were left shouting from the touchlines. Privately however he seemed almost to welcome his own death as a way of escape from exhausting predicaments.

London Review of Books, 1979

Sparks that Glowed

Memoirs. By Andrei Sakharov

Andrei Sakharov's life was of the stuff which makes legends – and makes them effective. Growing up in Russia at a time when there was starvation, terror, and the twisting of information for ideological ends, he nevertheless, as a physics student, by the time of the Second World War, had been dedicated enough, brilliant enough, to be part of a team making discoveries at the frontiers of quantum mechanics. By the 1950s he was the leading theorist in the construction of the Russian hydrogen bomb which was tested in 1953 – less than a year after the first American test. Sakharov had no regrets about his work on the Bomb – the world was still gripped in an atmosphere of war and it seemed to him essential that his country should have such weapons as were available. But almost immediately he began to campaign for the cessation of tests: scientists neither in America nor in Russia had not bargained for the extent of the effects of fall-out, and Sakharov argued that now some parity had been reached in powers of destruction, steps could be taken to pare these down. In this he was practical; he suffered from neither chauvinism nor guilt.

During the 1960s the banning of tests was his chief concern – together with a theoretical enquiry into the nature of the 'Big Bang' which was supposed to have occurred at the beginning of the universe. But by the 1970s his protests against the reluctance of Russian scientists (and indeed most scientists anywhere) to face global issues such as radioactive pollution had resulted in his being barred from the centre of research; he turned his attention to issues concerning human rights, about which his reputation as 'Father of the H-bomb' and 'Hero of Soviet Labour' ensured he would be heard. Just then his first wife died and he married Elena Bonner – herself a passionate fighter for human rights. It was then that the mainspring of his life moved out of the area of science and indeed out of conventional politics and into legend. He himself insisted that the force of the dissident movement was not pragmatic but moral. What could not easily be formulated was how a moral campaign, in a communist system, might be effective.

These *Memoirs* deal with nearly the whole of Sakharov's adult life, from 1921 to 1983 – he died in 1989. During the '80s he was virtu-ally under house arrest in internal exile in Gorky; he spent much of his time there working on the memoirs. His manuscripts were stolen, presumably by the KGB; once when he was in a dentist's chair (he tried always to carry his manuscripts with him); another time when they were snatched through a broken window from the back seat of his car. The *Memoirs* are written in a painstaking, transparently honest style that admits mistakes and faults; the transparency is such that a reader glimpses faults that the subject has not quite noticed himself. The whole book should be read as a story not just of a victim of Soviet oppression but of the way in which it is possible for an individual to take on the malignant, cumbersome apparatus of a communist state and, in a very evident sense, be effective.

As a human rights dissident Sakharov concentrated on individual instances of injustice – wrongful dismissals from jobs, imprisonments without trial, denials of the right to emigrate. He would write letters to whoever was the Russian leader of the time; he and his wife would turn up at trials and protest volubly; inevitably and increasingly they had to rely on foreign journalists for publicity. In 1968 Sakharov wrote an essay, *Reflections on Progress, Peaceful Co-existence and Intel-lectual Freedom*, which was published abroad: in this he extended his protests to warnings about 'the grave perils threatening the human race – thermonuclear extinction, ecological catastrophe, famine, an uncontrolled population explosion, alienation, and dogmatic distortion of our conception of reality'. He argued for '*convergence*, for a rapprochement of the socialist and capitalist systems that could eliminate or substantially reduce these dangers'. In this he fell out with Solzhenitsyn, who saw only decadence in the capitalist West and looked nostalgically to the past for an uncorrupted form of Rus-sian socialism. But it was Sakharov's acceptance of complexity, of the necessity for complementarity, that seemed – as it had done in the matter of the creation and then the banning of the H-bomb – to be in the true Russian tradition.

To an outsider the game played between Sakharov and the KGB in their efforts to silence his human rights protests (Sakharov often refers to it as a 'game') seems almost inexplicable: KGB agents dress up as telephone mechanics, as medical orderlies, as drunks; they break into his apartments and then wander out again; Sakharov declaims that their behaviour is 'contrary to the rule of law'. To an outsider there has been the impression that surely there is no rule of law! Yet here is Sakharov being harassed rather than eliminated: and inch by inch people in authority do seem to be paying attention to his protestations that there must be law. By this time he was a figure of international renown, and overt moves against him received hostile publicity. But still – no one had worried much about this in Stalin's day. It did seem that some morality was alive and spreading through a sort of osmosis.

One of the more resonant accounts tucked away in this vast and fascinating book is that of Sakharov in late middle age and while still barred from public activity, returning to his old enquiries into the stuff at the heart of matter; he dabbles in the fairy-tale world of protons and quarks and bosons and mesons – in which there is the reversibility of time, instantaneous action-at-a-distance, the experience of everything being connected to everything else. He is even drawn to the mysterious 'anthropic principle' in which it is suggested that necessarily 'our particular universe is distinguished by conditions favourable for the evolution of life and intelligence' just because of our ability to observe it and even thus in some sense to form it. This is the point at which top-flight physicists, to the annoyance of not-so-intelligent physicists, are apt to sound somewhat mystical. Sakharov at the beginning of this book denies that he is in a conventional sense 'religious', but he adds – 'Yet I am unable to imagine the universe and human life without some guiding principle, without a source of spiritual "warmth" that is non-material and not bound by physical laws'. It is this 'warmth' that in his later years Sakharov seems to have trusted – and to have been rewarded by.

In the meantime there have been times when his style of public protest does seem to become arbitrary and exaggerated: he goes on a hunger strike so that his stepson's fiancée might be given an exit visa for America; he vows to fast to death so that his adored wife can visit her children abroad and receive medical treatment there. Well-wishers say to him – 'You are harming your own cause by making stands on instances of not sufficient moment; you are hardening the intransigence of the authorities by making mountains out of commonplace bureaucratic molehills.' And often there was the accusation – 'It is your wife Elena Bonner who is the fanatic, who is leading you astray'. But always in the end Sakharov's reply was unanswerable: he had said that the fight for human rights was moral and not pragmatic; how better could morality be demonstrated than by fighting for those closest to one; how better could one demonstrate one's faith that thus morality might spread? He wrote -

Maybe I'm naive but . . . I began to believe that this wretched, downtrodden, corrupt and drunken people – no longer a *people* in any real sense of the word – is not yet entirely lost, not yet dead. The grandeur of Russia's history, the Orthodox religious revival, our role in revolutionary internationalism, may all seem unreal illusion when we contemplate today's Russia, but sparks of simple humanity and compassion for others have not yet been utterly extinguished. Will anything come out of them? For the nation as a whole, I have no idea, but is that so important? On the personal plane, I am certain that so long as there are people, the sparks will glow.

This was written in 1983. Sakharov was released from internal exile by a personal telephone call from President Gorbachev in December 1986. Since then sparks throughout the huge Soviet empire have glowed. Sakharov, before he died, must have known that he had been a Promethean carrier of fire.

Spectator, 1990

Cogs in Wheels

The New Sobriety: Art and Politics in the Weimar Period, 1917-33.
By John Willett

John Willett says he hopes his book will persuade readers 'first, that the arts are very closely interwoven with socio-political influences and ideas, and secondly, that this is not to be regretted, but at times can so stimulate the artists concerned as to produce results that from any point of view are highly original'. The period he takes to illustrate this thesis is that between the fading-out of the Dada and Expressionist movements in Europe after 1923, and the beginnings of Nazi power in 1930, which put a stop to artistic experiment. During this period there was in Germany what Mr Willett calls 'the new sobriety', when experimentation with artistic form was allied with left-wing political attitudes. At the centre of this was the Bauhaus, where artists and craftsmen came together to produce architecture and objects for use in daily life; also, numerous committees and organisations such as the Red Group, of which the chairman was George Grosz, dedicated to the production of politically committed painting.

John Willett's book is well-documented, and contains a mass of factual information about the movements and trends of art and artists during these years. It also provides an interesting and important corrective to the idea that art in Germany moved straight from what might be called the hangovers of Dada and Expressionism into the puritanical blind alley of Nazism. But the main thesis of the book – the suggestion that the 'new sobriety' was healthy and constructive – contains contradictions that Mr Willett seems to be aware of, but not to face.

The new sobriety was based on the idea that human beings only acquired dignity if they were looked upon as machines. 'Man isn't good, he's disgusting,' George Grosz announced. Werner Graeff wrote: 'Who cares about personality? We have buried all names, starting with our own'. The way in which man, individual man, could be made not disgusting, it was supposed, was by an immolation of himself as a cog in the social machine. There was an adulation of sport by artists of this time; not only because in getting fit for sport a man treated his body like a machine, but because sport was a form of expression appreciated by the proletarian masses.

The theatrical producer, Piscator, got the architect, Gropius, head of the Bauhaus, to build a gymnasium for him in his flat; Anton Raedderscheidt 'painted his big blond nudes toying with a tennis racket or swinging on the parallel bars, always observed by a gloomy man in a bowler hat'. (A critic wrote of such a woman that she 'from her splendidly trained flanks would now and again unleash a child as if driving a Slazenger ball with her racket'.) But while there was some sort of popular imagery to be found here in sport and machines, such artists for the most part seemed to be at home more in argument about art, in the grouping and regrouping of movements and committees, than in the production of imagery. This style indeed was akin to politics: the art that was produced was seldom memorable.

It has been a function of art traditionally to produce symbols that will represent not just this or that historical trend, but the fact that human consciousness can observe something of the nature of all trend-making, comic or tragic. This is a distinctive ability of being human. If art is allied too closely to ephemeral politics, then art loses its deeper function – and indeed politicians lose reminders of the larger context in which they exist.

Mr Willett claims: 'Our understanding of the arts becomes hopelessly narrowed as soon as "politics" is treated as a dirty word.' But in the next paragraph, he records how artists who strove to make politics a 'clean' word before 1933, afterwards were often arrested for political reasons and killed; and 'from then on Germany's pre-eminence was to be measured more in terms of tanks, aeroplanes, motorways, racing cars and uniformed blond men.' But what else might such artists have expected, when they had announced that human beings were of no interest except in so far as they were machines? A characteristic of machinery is that when parts of it do not perform the function for which they are built, they are expendable. If the state is a machine built of, and for, uniformed blond body-components, then artists and thinkers are apt to be dumped on the scrap-heaps of Dachau and Gulag. And even the more favoured members of society are apt to find themselves living as it were up a high-rise gum-tree.

The one undeniably major artist who is a central figure in this book is Brecht. Brecht had, or said he had, a total political commitment to Marxism; but what is interesting about Brecht (and, indeed, what seems to make him a major artist) is just that his stated political conviction is so little in evidence in his work. What is demonstrated in Brecht's plays is for the most part the ineffectuality of the prole-tariat as a mass: what is praised is individual human toughness and endurance. It is as if Brecht were saying: politics is, of course, a true subject-matter for art; but a true artist has to view his subject-matter truly; he may wish to be politically committed, but he has to see any commitment for what it is.

The other major artist who flits through these pages is Klee, who was a dedicated teacher in the Bauhaus for a time, but whose passion was not for politics but (in the words of his notes for a lecture of 1924) – 'to penetrate to the region of that secret place where primeval power nurses all evolution . . . in the womb of nature, at the source of creation, where the secret lies guarded'. Klee lived and worked in a political atmosphere, but as an artist he tried to portray the energies and drives that were behind all commitments and contexts. In this he is not unlike Brecht. Both artists, superficially so dissimilar, were concerned with looking through superficialities towards truth.

Listener, 1979

What Makes Life Worth Living

The Rape of Europe: the Fate of Europe's Treasures in the Third Reich and the Second World War. By Lynn H. Nicholas

A tale of the grim vicissitudes undergone by European artworks in the '30s and '40s might be expected to be depressing. In fact, what this book reveals is the extraordinary capacity for survival of objects that have the quality of inspiring devotion.

The story begins on a macabre note with the Nazis throwing out of their galleries, and sometimes destroying, what they called 'degenerate' art; by which was meant almost anything produced by a modern movement since the turn of the century. But such actions elicited a surprising reaction: people flocked to see and find sympathy with paintings that had been put on show to be mocked.

Later, when the war came and the Germans occupied much of Europe, there was widespread looting by the Nazis of such classical and Renaissance art as was held to be admirable – notably by agents acting for Hitler and Goering. Such appropriation was not without precedent: Napoleon had pillaged Europe to decorate Paris some 130 years before.

The pressures of war however resulted in these Nazi collections being hoarded rather than displayed, and thus preserved. They were placed in underground shelters to be safe from bombs and the attentions of further looters.

Architectural monuments that could not be moved nor much protected were the ones that suffered as the war swept across Europe. But for each act of savage and often needless destruction (the demolition of Russian churches by the Germans, the Allied bombing of Dresden), there can be found stories of almost miraculous preservation. In Paris, Rome, Florence, orders came down from higher authorities to destroy, but were disobeyed by people on the spot. And then when Allied forces began to reoccupy Europe there were the heroic efforts of the so-called 'Monuments Men' – British and American officers designated to point out what should not, if possible, be harmed in the heat of battle. Later their job was to discover and to identify the many thousands of artworks that had been stolen, mislaid, buried or otherwise hidden.

In the course of battle it was the natural instinct of fighting officers to safeguard the lives of their men, and sometimes there were mistakes and tragedies such as the bombing of the monastery at Monte Cassino. But even here it turned out that the Germans had sent to safety such artworks as could be moved. And at the end of the war the Monuments Men followed the trail of, and opened up, one abundant treasure-trove after another.

Curators of museums and private collections had gone to remarkable lengths to protect and carry to safety objects they loved; packing materials had to be improvised, and transport commandeered. The man who had taken on the task of looking after the Mona Lisa had insisted that he himself travel in its hermetically sealed container, and had nearly died of asphyxiation.

Most of the works had been taken to the cellars of country houses or to the shafts of mines; there, makeshift but successful methods had been set up to maintain the right temperature and humidity. What is amazing is how very few paintings at the very top level were lost – a Raphael portrait, a Bellini Madonna and Child, Signorelli's *Pan*, Mantegna's frescoes at Padua. Some stories of survival have the style of a thriller: there is a photograph reproduced here of Leonardo's *Lady with the Ermine* being 'liberated' from her nondescript packing case by armed soldiers in a railway siding.

The story is heartening because it shows that in spite of the appalling prevalence of human rapacity, duplicity, greed and self-destruction, there are people who dedicate their lives not only to producing works of art but also to preserving them, even when others seem intent on devastation. The artworks themselves, of course, have a hand in this: they are expressions of that which can make life worthwhile.

Daily Telegraph, 1994

PART IV
Philosophy and Practice

From *Journey into the Dark*, III

A concomitant of the vogue for deconstruction in the second half of the twentieth century has been the so-called information explosion – that burgeoning of presentations of fact or fancy which can offer, through electronic technology, almost infinite material for stupefaction under the light. At the touch of a button or two there can come up on a screen – almost anything, that is the point. You can scrounge and be fed haphazardly, or you can get a version of what you ask for – but you cannot ask for what you do not know, and how will you learn to discriminate as you have to do in the dark? You can be bemused or you can be gratified by what you imagine you desire; but by this you will not be nudged from your prejudices and predilections nor from the confines of a game. Lovers of the Internet are like pinball players who shunt balls here and there beneath the protection of a glass screen: they click machinery and lights come on and balls drop into holes; but what chance has the machinery to bump into, to come up against, anything to affect them?

One deconstructionist or post-deconstructionist critic who has seen the implications of the information explosion is the French *savant* Jean Baudrillard. He writes – 'Information devours its own contents. . . . Instead of causing communication, it exhausts itself in staging communication: instead of producing meaning, it exhausts itself in staging meaning' (*In the Shadow of the Silent Majorities*). Consumers of information summon apparitions by the waving of a wand: but it is the aim of a magician that there shall be no distinction between true and false: the skill is to beguile, and what is real has no relevance. A television audience watches a political argument or a presentation of events as if these were a theatrical performance or sport – to be evaluated in terms of whether illusion has been successful, or who has come out on top. 'The medium and the real are now in a single nebulous state in which truth is indecipherable'. Baudrillard sees this partly as a catastrophe in the usual sense – a condition in which there is no concept of responsibility or authenticity: 'a winding down to the bottom of a circle leading to what can be called "the horizon of the event"; to the horizon of meaning beyond which one cannot go'.

But just because of the extremity of this, Baudrillard suggests, there may be some paradoxical effect – in the way in which (though leading to a different outcome) the vogue for deconstruction might have given at least to some individuals the impetus to look at themselves. If people in the mass, that is, submit long enough to the bedazzlement of information, then some form of snow-blindness may set in; as a result of which they may find themselves willy-nilly in the dark. And then, might there become available some operation of grace?

What Baudrillard suggests is a curious reversal of the common image of a passive mass audience inert in front of its computers or television screens being manipulated by a media or a business élite intent on its own power and prestige. Is it not rather, he proposes, that a mass audience has become like some gigantic queen ant or queen bee – a static and apparently semi-moribund presence but one being served by frenetic gangs of would-be champions and workers who depend for their own existence on honouring it and keeping it alive. The masses may seem powerless and to have no choice; but they are formidable in that others seem only able to make choices in terms of what they, the masses, might want. Baudrillard writes –

> The masses know they know nothing and have no desire to know. The masses know they are powerless and they don't want power. We reproach them vigorously for these signs of stupidity and passivity; but they are not like that at all; the masses are very snobbish. They act like Brummel and sovereignly delegate the faculty of choice to someone else – in a sort of game of irresponsibility, of ironic challenge, of secret ruse. All mediators (political, intellectual, heirs to the philosophers of the Enlightenment in their contempt for the masses) are only good basically for this: to administer by delegation, by proxy, this tedious business of power and will, to relieve the masses of this transcendence for their greater pleasure, and then to reward them with the spectacle of it. (*Fatal Strategies*)

(The mention of Beau Brummel refers to an occasion when he was confronted with a spectacular landscape and was asked which was his favourite lake. He turned to his valet and said 'Which do I prefer?')

This vision of the masses as an effete but stylish aristocrat around whom publicists and politicians fawn does have relevance in this increasingly unconscious age in which in counterpoint to the infantilism and deceits and corruptions of those in public life there does seem to be some faint sanity miraculously preserved, or how does any orderliness exist at all? Democracy does still seem to be the most tolerable form of government perhaps just because the voting masses do not seem to pay much attention to the rubbish that is hurled at them by politicians; they have more contempt for politicians than politicians can afford to have for them: some instinct seems to stay alive through their near-inoperancy in the light. But 'ironic challenge'; 'secret ruse'? Some fecund saving grace may move in its own way in the dark; but if any self-consciousness is to be found within the queen bee's passive gestation – if anything is to be skilful in the 'winding down' to the bottom of the circle of light where recognition might flip over on to another arena – then surely it will be in a different style, of a different nature, to that of scurrying servants or torpid queens. It will have to be, in this doctored world, something with energy and function arising from a pregnant awareness of and within itself. In the journey into the dark one looks for oneself and one's not-self; one stretches out a hand and finds a hand stretched out; this may lead to a discovery that is like the birth of a child. Children seem naturally to see the grown-up world as mad: maybe they see their own antics as mad – but at least they have fun with these as goblins or tricksters or buffoons. Then they grow up – and either join grown-ups in pretending that they are not mad, or embark on further journeys. And for these they will have to nurture and practise, as it is incumbent on children to do if they are to stay sane in this abusive world, some 'ironic challenge'; 'secret ruse'. These will depend on luck and skill, which in turn will depend on each other – as can be learned in a journey into the dark.

Some twenty years ago I tried to say what I felt about power and powerlessness; of irony and secrecy and ruse –

> There is enough evidence nowadays, goodness knows that it is the conventionally powerful people who seem slavish – those politicians, pundits, leaders of the fashionable world who in their uniformity of livery and adherence to strict routines and in their inability to behave as they might like on the spur of any moment not only look like servants and behave like servants but (don't be taken in by this!) really are public servants – those bewigged and bewildered figures caught sleepless on the steps of aeroplanes; their bags under their eyes like suitcases; always ready to jump to the call of a microphone or a bell; on the trot from dawn to long after dusk; hardly any time to see their loved ones; their engagement books filled for months and even years; and always liable, like soldiers emerging from a wood, to be taken hostage or shot – such vulnerabilities extending to their children and their children's children. These are the people who are honoured socially

now; who have power; who choose to live like this – this is the point – no one makes them. And the people who choose to try to be able to do as they like, to look for what it is that they like, who discover that this often involves them in difficult (but pleasurable?) rejections of that to which they have become accustomed – these are people held with little social honour in the modern world; who perhaps on some level are envied, but not always enough to stop making themselves and others happy.

What has hitherto been objectionable about élites has just been the assumption that such people should have power. But if the word is taken away from the concept of power – if it is recognised that it is now the powerful people who seem slavish and the only true concept of an élite would be that of people who in this sense are specifically non-privileged – then what would be the harm? For everyone – both privileged and non-privileged – pays at least lip-service to the overriding value of freedom; and what would be objectionable about an élite which most people who had the choice could not bear to be part of?

Certainly someone trying to hold himself on the side of a non-privileged élite should have no illusions about his involvement with trying to keep in balance different parts of himself; to feel himself simple and all-of-a-piece would be to fail. He must be handling both aloofness and the social cunning to remain aloof; holding on, and not too tightly, to something fluttering, like a bird. As soon as success was grasped it would have to be freed: the mark of success would be something continually changing to stay the same. It would be like a child, to be fostered, to grow; but to live its own life: to be both held, and not held, at once. To learn to love oneself would be like tending a seed, a pearl (as has been said): a matter of skill however much also of luck: the ability to take advantage of luck (and indeed of non-luck): a making the best, and something profitable, of what it is that comes one's way: but what comes is usually averaged, and so one has a choice.

(*Catastrophe Practice*, 1979)

Unpublished, 1998

A Question of Probabilities

John Maynard Keynes: Volume Two – the Economist as Saviour 1920-1937. By Robert Skidelsky

The great merit of the first volume of Robert Skidelsky's biography of Keynes was the way it combined the portrait of the Bloomsbury aesthete with that of the man of affairs – the sophistication of one side of Keynes influencing the other – so that, for instance, he was able to protest with authority against the self-destructively punitive measures of the Treaty of Versailles.

In this second volume Keynes the economist separates himself from Bloomsbury. He never gives up his interest in the arts, but this becomes focused on the career of his wife, the ballerina and actress Lydia Lopokova, and aesthetics gives way to the preoccupation with economics. The resulting technicalities pose a problem for the biographer. Robert Skidelsky formulates some of the more abstruse doctrines in appendices to his chapters, but if the main story is to be valid there is no escape from a plunge into the deep end of economic theory. It is the merit of this volume that a general reader never quite loses a hand-hold at the edge of this murky pool, and there is some fascination in the spectacle of experts so antagonistically splashing and pushing one another under.

In his Bloomsbury days Keynes had dabbled in philosophy. He wrote *A Treatise on Probability*, in which he argued that although forecasts in practical affairs could not suggest certainty, there could nevertheless be a rational assessment of risks. This idea remained at the back of his evolving ideas about economics. Against the laissez-faire orthodoxy (that for a healthy capitalist society markets had to be allowed to go their own ways) Keynes argued that the escalating pattern of boom and slump would, if left to itself, run the risk of invoking a far more dangerous form of government interference than that which he was advocating: if capitalism was not to collapse into communism or fascism, that is, there would have to be government intervention by means of investment and control of rates of interest. The success of such manipulation would depend on the virtuosity of those who administered it.

Keynes's principal work, *General Theory of Employment, Interest and Money*, published in 1936, suggested the rules for such manipulation. Behind the technicalities was the recommendation that people and communities should invest rather than save; consume rather than hoard. The orthodox idea had been that one saved in order to invest so that consumption might increase at a later date: Keynes warned that the time-lag involved in this would result in economic stagnation: much more effective would be a decision to encourage consumption now which would result in demand and thus in the quick attraction of investment. The main social problem of the 1930s was unemployment: saving increased unemployment; spending alleviated it. Inflation might be avoided if the money supply was manipulated cleverly rather than simply increased.

The technical arguments that still rage about Keynes's *General Theory* are about how, and indeed whether, such manipulation might be done. If Skidelsky will lose the attention of one or two general readers here this is because the experts, with their contorted disagreements, seem to lose each other. The great flaw in economic theory is the assumption that human beings are rational; theorists themselves all too often demonstrate that rationality can be at odds with itself.

Keynes never lost sight of the realisation that successful outcomes to economic problems depend fundamentally on states of mind. Economics is a moral business as much as a rational one: it is to do with risk-taking and the assessment of risks; with optimism, courage, 'animal spirits', breadth of vision. In this he was demonstrating once more the fruits of his Bloomsbury background.

Keynes made a lot of money himself, and he helped his old Bloomsbury friends with money. They never renounced their friendship with him, though they complained of his growing worldliness and that of his wife. Lydia, with her ebullience and her malapropisms ('Jesus fomenting wine out of water at Cannes') emerges as the heroine of this book. Keynes himself in his personal life was apt to put his theories about expenditure into exaggerated effect: he overworked, overconsumed, and had a serious heart attack at the age of fifty-three.

Skidelsky speaks of Keynes setting out to save capitalism – a system he had some contempt for, but which he saw as the best available for making possible a good life. A final judgement about how far he succeeded must wait for the third and last volume – perhaps till the history of the twenty-first century is written. Keynes seems to have been right about many of his short-term recommendations. He glimpsed the long-term ecological dangers of extreme consumption, but thought these could only anyway be countered by population control; he also admitted the possibly debilitating effects of a society depending for its welfare on manipulation and tricks. He lamented to Virginia Woolf that their generation had had the benefits of a religious background as well as those of overthrowing it; the next generation might find themselves equipped with nothing but tricks.

Much of the fascination of this book is the way that so many of its themes are echoed today (1992). Arguments in 1915 about the Gold Standard are much the same as those about the Exchange Rate Mechanism: there is still the balancing act between unemployment and inflation, the choice between stability and risk. It still seems the best hope for capitalism is that it should be explained and when possible manipulated by persons of virtuosity and wide sympathies – such as Keynes or indeed the author of this book. For the rest, the possibilities remain beyond the range of rational assessment.

Daily Telegraph, 1992

The Enemy of Paradox

Bertrand Russell: The Spirit of Solitude. By Ray Monk

This is the first volume of an already impressive biography that succeeds in presenting Bertrand Russell's philosophical work, his political commitments and his highly intricate emotional life in an interweaving narrative. Russell emerges as a figure of bizarre inconsistency, but of such demonic and creative energy that his bouts of inhumanity seem to be redeemed. Ray Monk's achievement is not to judge, but to let the story comprehensively speak for itself.

Both Russell's parents were dead by the time he was four. He grew up a solitary child in a house dominated by a sanctimonious grandmother; he learned there was madness in the family; he feared he might go mad himself. Sanity seemed to depend on a search for inner certainty. In his early twenties he became a Fellow of Trinity College, Cambridge, and from this vantage point he set out to find in logic and mathematics a system of demonstrable objective truths. In logic he eventually came up against the blank wall of paradox – that of the Cretan who says all Cretans are liars; of the barber (this was Russell's particular formulation) who shaves everyone in the village who does not shave himself – so if he does he doesn't and if he doesn't he does. There was also difficulty with sentences that philosophers like to play with such as 'The present King of France is bald' – but since there is no present King of France then he neither is bald nor does he have hair – and so on. Russell's hope that he was finding something about reality by such weird games was exploded finally by Wittgenstein who proposed that truths in such an area could not be stated but only shown: the proposition for instance 'There is not a rhinoceros in this room' could not be proved nor disproved logically. Shortly after this Wittgenstein and Russell went their different ways – Wittgenstein to silence or to ruminate on what, if anything, might still be said beyond games with words: Russell increasingly to politics and to efforts to change the world.

In the meantime however he and A. N. Whitehead had produced their monumental three-volumed *Principia Mathematica* which was an attempt to present indubitable truths in mathematical symbols if not in words. By the middle of the second volume they had managed to produce a proof that two plus two did in fact equal four; but after this the process of proof became more difficult, and Russell himself admitted 'I know of only six people who have read the later parts of the book'. And some twenty years later the mathematician Gödel produced his generally accepted and proven theory that in fact all logical theories of mathematics are destined to be incomplete.

Russell as a young man suffered from fierce sexual frustration and he seems to have married his first wife, Alys, largely in order to allay this. But in his yearning for any form of certainty he was driven to dress up his desires in wild romantic imagery; this did not hinder him however when desires were satisfied from treating his lovers with alarming cold-ness. He embarked on a long love-affair with Ottoline Morrell; they played a complex game of intermingling the sexual with the spiritual – of renunciation and rapturous reconciliation. At this stage Russell seldom had fewer than two or three mistresses concurrently available. Letters whizzed to and fro occasioning as much confusion as that caused by the bewildered village barber or the bald French king.

By the time of the First World War, Russell was active in politics on behalf of women's suffrage, against conscription, in favour of a negotiated peace. In 1918 his protests led him to spend a few months in prison which, he said, gave him a chance to get back to philoso-phy. But when he emerged he found himself fêted as a champion of socialism; so he visited communist Russia, which he hated, and still feudal China, which he loved – thus finding himself once more in a position of confronting paradox.

Ray Monk manages to make Russell's philosophy largely intelligible at least to the point where Russell began to find it unintelligible himself. But Monk understandably can find little orderliness in the prevarications of Russell's love-life, and some numbness is induced by the story of convoluted repetitions. But by the end of this first volume – in 1921 when Russell is forty-nine and has just married his second wife Dora and has had his first child – it is difficult for a reader not to be somewhat awe-struck at his dedication in his fevered search for certainty. While he was struggling with the problems of logical paradox he had come up with a theory of a hierarchy of different 'logical types' – the theory that a statement which refers to a fact is of a lower logi-cal type than one which refers to another statement, or to a class of things, or indeed to itself. But for all his theorising and rhapsodising

Russell never seems to have achieved any feasible view of himself. He did however from time to time return to an early haunting insight – that what he was searching for was that which in various manifestations had often been called God. Russell did not like what he saw of Christianity: but it is striking that the words he used to describe his occasional experiences of certainty, of what might be called 'holiness', were that they were like a 'passionate love for a Ghost'.

Daily Telegraph, 1996

The Moral Voluptuousness of Hell

The Passion of Michel Foucault. By James Miller
The Lives of Michel Foucault. By David Macey

Last year Didier Eribon published a biography of Michel Foucault which proclaimed him to be one of the great philosophers of the twentieth century, but did not make it easy to see why. Foucault had turned upside down ideas about the distinction between sanity and madness; had proposed that systems of law and order were little more than arbitrary structures imposed by the self-interests of society. Such suggestions had great appeal to French and American intellectuals and students in the '70s, not least because their unintelligibility made them easy for deconstructionists to play with.

Here are two more biographies which try to explain Foucault more deeply. James Miller, an American, does this by relating Foucault's work to his life. David Macey, an Englishman, acknowledges peculiarities in the life, but is of the school that believes that an author should be understood only through an ever more detailed examination of his work.

In *The Passion of Michel Foucault* James Miller looks at the philosopher's obsession with death, his toying with hallucinatory drugs and suicide, his plunge towards the end of his life into rituals of extreme sadomasochism. It is an understanding of this, Miller claims, that can give a shape to the work. Foucault is proposing that the true nature of humans is not to be responsible for bringing order out of chaos, but to go to some limiting extreme of a natural disorder – to find an almost mystical apotheosis where life and death, pain and pleasure, meet. Foucault died of AIDS at the age of 57. It is suggested that the path leading to AIDS might have been an almost willed self-destruction; the rotting of the body freeing some approach to spirituality.

Miller's book is seductive and easily readable: there are accounts of the bizarre goings-on in the homosexual 'bath-houses' of San Francisco. Questions about the extent of the relevance of such so-called 'private' life to an author's work are dramatically posed; but they remain questions.

In *The Lives of Michel Foucault* David Macey is more scholarly in dealing with Foucault's political involvement in the various protest movements of the '70s, his public wrangles with other intellectuals, his lectures and occasional writings. But when it comes to clarifying the contents of the main books he is no more successful than others have been. These books challenged and indeed knocked down some accepted notions about rationality and authority – but then what remained? Foucault seemed to suggest that his aim was to celebrate 'the disappearance of man'; 'the liquidation of the principle of identity'. But there he was himself – a startling identity.

The reader confronting these two biographies is thus left with a choice – to watch with Macey while the philosophical work seems to drift away in fireworks and smoke, or to agree with Miller that if connections between the life and the work are accepted, then there are still some interesting things to be said.

Reports of the appalling cruelties that go on in the outside world (as in, say, Bosnia) make it difficult to deny that the lust for cruelty, and the lust for excitement through hardship involving pain, lie deep within human nature; they are not just the product of faulty social customs. Foucault makes the point that such drives are at the back of much social organisation – we get satisfaction from the imposition of legal restrictions and the infliction of punishment. The dream of the Enlightenment that humans might grow to be peaceable and rational, the dream of the Marxists that humans might be organised to be free – these have failed. For 100 years the most powerful prophetic voices in the West have been saying that it is only by recognising the drive to affliction and disorder in human nature that any chance of liveliness may be liberated – and this may involve some closeness to death.

Miller quotes Nietzsche: 'The path to one's own heaven always leads through the voluptuousness of one's own hell.' Apart from the 'voluptuousness' there is a Christian idea of purgation here; and it is significant that at the end of Foucault's life, when he was plunging towards AIDS, he was involved in scholarly research into the disciplines of confession and penance as practised by early Christians – the idea of salvation through self-exposure and suffering.

A Christian, of course, would see the sadomasochistic side of man as part of his fallen nature, though it might indeed be by the facing of this that there might be a return to wholeness. Foucault accepted such a vision, writing:

> The Christian ascetic struggled with a diabolical double, conjuring up this demonic other in order to defeat and drive out, through a kind of spiritual combat, this despicable self.

The use of the word 'despicable' is surprising: Foucault usually saw his task as the giving of due respect to all sides of human nature. But he did not get beyond a view of the successful outcome of this being some glorious death-by-immolation: he had no sense of what he called a 'limit-experience' resulting in any form of new or on-going life.

Daily Telegraph, 1993

Philosophy Back in the Mainstream?

Metaphysics as a Guide to Morals. By Iris Murdoch

This is a roller-coaster of a book, a journey through philosophy, religion, literature, art – less a guide than a gigantic survey, a mapping, providing readers with the means to find their own ways. This form is deliberate: metaphysics and morals do not constitute areas within which simple pathways can be drawn; landscapes can be presented within which individuals choose.

Philosophers have always seen as a problem the differentiation between facts and morals: 'is' has no self-evident connection with 'ought'. As a result morals have got shunted out of the main lines of philosophy. One of Miss Murdoch's points is that by doing this philosophy has often shunted itself out of the mainstream of life.

In reality, our everyday perception of 'facts' are to do with evaluation and thus with morals: we make a choice to give our attention to this fact rather than that. If we try to give reasons for such processes then we have the problem of giving reasons for our reasons – and so on, in infinite regression. It is because of this that modern philosophers have suggested that areas of metaphysics and morals are outside the proper bounds of philosophy; they are within the less restrictive regions of religion, literature, art.

The background to Miss Murdoch's philosophy is provided by Plato, who was aware of the limitations of the written word but who suggested that 'truth' could be approached through discourse: to every answer there was another question, but at the end of the to-and-fro of discourse some understanding might have been conveyed. In Plato's image of humans facing the wall of a cave there are three stages in the apprehension of reality: there is awareness of the shadows, of the objects that cast the shadows, and then of the sun. Movement from one to the other implies a spiritual journey.

Other figures from traditional philosophy that loom large in this book are Kant, who saw that morals were inseparable from some acceptance of transcendence; and Schopenhauer, who suggested that a higher level of reality might be glimpsed through works of art. Of more modern thinkers there are Wittgenstein, who suggested that when the limits of traditional philosophy had been reached (quite quickly in his *Tractatus*) there should be philosophic silence; Heidegger, who agreed that at this point philosophy and morality should depend on doing rather than on talking; and Simone Weil, who proposed that a moral journey, after the emptying of the self, depended on a careful *attentiveness* to the outside world. In all of this there is the pattern of a spiritual journey to seek something that is never perhaps quite found, but which is learned by virtue of the journey. In this sense we are all like artists. Miss Murdoch sums this up -

> Truth is found by 'truthful' endeavour; both words are needed in a just description of language. Truth is learned, found, in specialised areas of art where the writer (for instance) struggles to make his deep intuitions of the world into artful, truthful judgements. . . . The world is not given to us 'on a plate', it is given to us as a creative task. It is impossible to banish morality from this picture. We *work,* using or failing to use our honesty, our courage, our truthful imagination, at the interpretation of what is present to us, as we of necessity shape it and 'make something of it'.

This passage comes at the end of a criticism of modern 'structuralist' theory, which holds that there is no validity in the idea that a writer might have been searching for anything; there is only the text – and the availability of this for critics to play with. But this theory is a *trahison des clercs* – the withdrawal of intellectuals from areas of morality and meaning so that merchants of power go uncriticised on their way. As Miss Murdoch puts it – 'Here the severance of meaning from truth, and language from the world, can be seen as not only philosophically baseless and morally intolerable, but as politically suicidal'.

I know of no other writer who could have covered such large areas with such authority, nor had the courage to treat fashions with such disdain. But perhaps it is the result of admiration for Miss Murdoch's great gifts that there is at the end of this book, for all its energy and scope, some disappointment – as indeed can be felt at the end of some of even her most striking novels. These are wondrous surveys; but at the end do readers have to be quite so ruthlessly abandoned by their guide?

Miss Murdoch comes to an acceptance of the idea of God as a result of her spiritual journey – transcendence is discovered as a result of attention to immanence. But then she also is haunted by the overwhelming prevalence of evil: she writes, 'There can be no pact between good and evil, they are irreconcilable enemies . . . there is no harmonious balance whereby we suddenly find that evil is just a "dark side" which is not only harmless to good but actually enhances it'. This is why, perhaps, for her, things have to be said to remain accidental – in spite of her endeavours and her displays that they need not be. Miss Murdoch in her religion appears more Buddhist than Christian. In Buddhism the world remains remorselessly within the encirclement of nothingness or evil: in Christianity it is believed that some pattern between good and evil is, however inharmoniously, being worked out – both within an individual and in the history of the world.

Daily Telegraph, 1992

Part V
Religion

The Church and Art

In the days when humans were naturally religious and the Church was the form in which a religious society was ordered, artists were just skilled workers, people who made things, who worked for the glory of God. They were anonymous craftsmen and their work was anonymous. They either glorified God by the proper making of a properly useful object or, if they wished to be more specific, by making an object of praise, or one to show the meaning of God and man as understood in the history of the Creation. They built a cathedral, or illustrated a manuscript, or made some other offering of worship.

After the Reformation – after religion became less a matter of offering the works of one's daily life to God and became more a matter of faith seeming to justify whatever were one's predilections – persons who wished to express by their craft something of life's meaning now found traditional religious models less natural to work from. Thus a tribe of 'artists' arose who were no longer ordinary workmen but specialists in the field of the pursuit and expression of significance; and this was to be found in the artist's vision of the world around him. Representational painting became fashionable, with portraiture and historical scenes and landscape. There was still however the impression that what was being looked for and represented was something sacred.

In the present day not only have the things of the world become split off from the things of the spirit, but there is little imagination that the Godless world possesses a form and meaning of its own. Thus in a world given over largely to the exercise of power and the pursuit of money, an artist who seeks to express meaning is driven for the most part to jokiness or savagery. And the churchman, who believes he still knows meanings as ordained by God, finds he is trying to convey them by means that are unintelligible to others.

But art is that which can convey meaning to those who by the circumstances of their lives might not be readily disposed to see it.

The Church grew, and spread, by means of art. The parables of

Jesus, for instance, are art. They are short stories. They tell of things that can be told in no better way. The effect on the hearer or reader depends not upon argument nor reason, but upon their nature and quality as stories.

The Gospels are works of art. They are not biographies, nor histories, but impressions by writers, the validity of which does not depend upon historical proof, but upon the reader's experience of their authority.

The Epistles are art. They are written in a burgeoning style, and it is this that holds the attention and conveys the meaning. St Paul himself said, 'Let your speech always be gracious, seasoned with salt, so that ye may know how you ought to answer everyone'. This was a recognition of the function of art.

In the great ages of the Church its language was that of art. The story of God and man was written in poems, and declared and sung and painted. The mass of people were brought up and learned their faith by listening to inspired words and music and looking at inspiring illustrations. The understanding of Christianity was thus scattered like seeds. The Christian life was lived, and uttered, in the light of an understanding that things had meaning. The meaning was conveyed by the style. The two, as art, were inseparable.

Philosophers tell us that logically metaphysics is meaningless. But the experience of art is that metaphysics are not meaningless.

If the churchman of today wishes to get back his voice and means of action it is just this that he has to recognise – what is the nature of art and what are its disciplines. He has to recognise that art is the proper language of metaphysics; it is by this alone that the meanings of 'being' and 'knowing' can be conveyed. It is what can still speak when reason has to be silent.

The disciplines of art are the same as those of religion – that you not only have to believe in it but to live it. It is this that will deter-mine 'style' and 'authority'. The authority of a religious man depends upon his integrity – the conjunction of what he believes and what he does. The authority of an artist will depend upon a conjunction of what he most deeply knows and what with most dedication and effort he makes – and this is what will result in the style that conveys his meaning. Words and representations without style are evanescent; art gives them the tensions and paradoxes within which the truths of eternity are caught. Every man is a particular kind of artist: everyone has something to do, or to make, in the life to which he is called. Art comes from the true pains he takes in doing it.

For the churchman who does not know how to be reassured in or to communicate his belief, this, then, is one of the first things to do

– to make things, to build, for the glory of God, out of his own heart and his experience. He has to live what he believes and then express it. He must make his churches once more things of beauty which will be illustrative and instructive of the meaning of God and man; his service must be offerings of songs and poetry that will be again living symbols of praise and thanksgiving. His symbols will live if he is living his faith; and it is by them, also, that his faith will spread in the world around him.

And he will find, if he does this, that he is doing something for himself. Often, nowadays, the churchman does not know what communal actions are demanded of him: he prays, and tries to love his neighbours, but in corporate gestures he is feeble. He may feel he has to 'prove' his faith: but this is not what faith requires. By turning his attention to his expressions of worship, to the style and beauty of his songs and prayers and of the buildings and objects around him, he will be giving himself and his community enough to exercise them for a lifetime. And because he will be working for God's sake, whatever else turns up may fall into place.

Prism, 1959

Through a Glass Darkly

When I was young I was an agnostic and indeed anti-Christian on the usual grounds – where was the evidence for a loving God in a world of such cruelty and senselessness? But then I, seeing the world in this way, seemed to be becoming senseless and somewhat destructive too. Then through an old friend, and a sense of loyalty to him, I met a holy man – Father Raymond Raynes, an Anglican monk of the Community of the Resurrection – and it seemed to me he spoke with authority, he spoke what was true; he spoke about what was not senseless. His style was so tentative that it was almost as if it were not himself speaking, but he were paying attention to something speaking through him. He said that the world was indeed senseless if one saw it as senseless; but there was a way of seeing that it was not, if one chose to try this.

I had the experience of some enlightenment: but I was still the person I was. After some years of doubt and digging in my toes it seemed that I would have to make some commitment to what Father Raynes represented if I was to have a chance of finding out more about sense. So I decided to try to follow some rule of life that I understood was traditional – I went to church, took communion, struggled with prayer, made my confession, became a churchwarden in my local church. For a time I even gave up writing novels – a profession that I loved, but which seemed to be causing me confusion, in that I did not see how one could have the openness and readiness to embrace all kinds of experience necessary to write good novels if one was trying to lead a religiously 'good' life. I was offered, and accepted, the editorship of a small, supposedly iconoclastic and avant-garde, religious magazine called *Prism*. For this I wrote fervent articles in the style of a recently converted devotee.

None of this came easily to me; it was like some ordeal. But it continued to seem a necessary ordeal, in that one was geared in to a process of learning.

Then eventually as part of this commitment, and during a bout of illness, I read the Bible straight through, which as it happens Christians do not usually do; they are in the habit of diverting its effect by reading it chopped up in bits and pieces. But from reading it as a whole, a pattern of understanding emerged which I had not expected.

The Bible seemed to be saying – Once upon a time there was an effort by humans to understand God (or if you like, an effort by God to make himself understood by humans) by living according to rules, and this is the story told in the Old Testament. But the effort to do this failed, and the story ended in darkness and confusion.

Then there was a second attempt by God to give humans a chance to understand what they were for (or if you like, a new effort by humans to understand this) and this was the story of the New Testament. In this humans were told that, yes, they had to try to observe rules; but being human they would often fail. Such failure however would not weigh so much in the balance as their ability to admit this and bear it. For if they did admit it, and looked at their situation truly, then in fact the job of salvation had been, or could be, or was being, done for them. They had to have faith, that is, in the operations of God as manifested in Jesus Christ, and this would be a not impossible form of obedience.

But then at the very end of the Gospel stories there was a further suggestion – that if one recognised all this, then one might move beyond efforts at these probably necessary but not-quite-grown-up forms of obedience, and become oneself a partaker in the business of salvation and redemption. This could be done through the agency of the Holy Spirit. Towards the end of St John's Gospel Jesus suggests that soon his disciples should be paying attention not so much to Himself as to the God that will be within them as well as outside them. He says –

> It is expedient for you that I go away, for if I do not go away, the Comforter will not come unto you; but if I will depart, I will send him unto you . . .
>
> Howbeit when he, the Spirit of Truth, is come, he will guide you into all truth; for he will not speak of himself; but of whatsoever he shall hear, that shall he speak; and he will show you things to come.

This riddling utterance (necessarily riddling because it requires that each person shall listen for its meaning) seemed to me clearly to mean – however beautiful and still necessary are childish observances, you can move on, and watch and listen for manifestations and requirements of the Spirit. These will be in the everyday world outside you; they will be available to you through that which has grown inside you.

With regard to my own story – to be sure there were still sad patterns. But these did not now seem to be entirely senseless nor stricken with failure, but rather challenges to be worked through. I did not regret the sometimes fervid style of my early writing for *Prism*: there is a time for ardour. And after a time I went back to writing my books, my novels – in which I could try to express my understanding now of how in spite of sadness and absurdity things did, if you trusted them, seem to work themselves out with great subtlety and wonder.

From a talk in Balliol College Chapel, 1994

A Social Contract?

The social abuses of this age and country are not primarily practical ones of injustice and squalor, but more ones of the spirit, or psyche, manifested personally and in the community. This is the age of untruthfulness, of double-think, of loss of integrity and a profound lack of courage. It is not nowadays that we are deliberately wicked; we are simply mad. The significance of our attitude towards such things as the H-bomb, apartheid, Suez, doesn't lie in our wrongness about them (to such questions there can properly be two sides) but rather that even on our own sides we do not make sense. Everyone told lies about Suez; few admit their real feelings about apartheid; about the H-bomb we are frivolous as hysterics. What the world has now denied is the importance of truthfulness and integrity and honour. We are in a moral vacuum, with no values, and the idols of publicity are in the place of God.

All this, of course, is not definable in terms of reason or statistics. It perhaps has to be sensed (in so far as it is true) on the same level as that on which it was once felt there was something wrong with slavery, with the burning of witches, or with sweated child labour. These things were not faced by theologians, but by people who perhaps just used their eyes and ears and then went back to their New Testaments and at some stage thought – *there's something wrong here somewhere*. They put two and two together by a sort of arithmetic of the imagination – and even then could not prove that their sums were true, but could only exhort others to go through the same disciplines of imagination.

The one half of this sum nowadays are the formal expressions of inanity on TV, in the press, in MP's speeches, advertising, conversations both at dinner parties and pubs; also the informal effect of these things which is perhaps seen in the apathy if not yet in the corruption of more humdrum forms of society. And the other half of the sum is, as always, what God has told us of righteousness in the world – of the means of grace in daily living. And if the two halves are put together then, I think, the result is a disparity so shocking that one has to try to take a stand against it.

Because the present abuses are those of dissimulation and moral chaos, then our remedies must be in this sphere – in a concentration not on political nor social lobbying but on demonstrations personally and in groups of what a Godly life of integrity could be. And I don't believe that this attitude encourages a retreat into unworldliness: in fact I believe the opposite – that it is an emphasis on polemics and political accusation that results in unreality, and an emphasis on spiritual courage results in social witness.

Can there be an effect in the practical world via the spiritual? I don't *want* to believe this, because it is disturbing and imposes a considerable strain on one's meagre spiritual resources; one cannot easily knock off and take a rest. But I do believe that the spiritual courage and integrity of a hermit, say, in Battersea can in fact change the heart or alleviate the sufferings of a crippled criminal in Peckham; and I believe this because I think it is what the Christian faith is about, in distinction from the old Jewish law. And what other way is there of demonstrating one's belief in that wholly vital but at the moment apparently forgotten Person of Western Christendom – the Holy Spirit?

Prism, 1959

For Heaven's Sake – Repent!

The central act of Christianity is one of sacrifice.

Today in England the facade that the church presents is one of a vested interest in patterns of mind and habit in which people to whose advantage it is to be churchmen are churchmen and those to whom there is no advantage are not. By 'advantage' I mean the chance to satisfy a desire for a function or a hobby in society in the manner most gratifying to the person's character and tastes. People seem to 'belong' to the church for the same reasons that solicitors are solicitors; or members of a pop-singer's fan-club hang together around stage doors.

It is this appearance of the church that explains its almost total lack of contact with any part of the country's life except its own. It is imagined to be something in the nature of a trades-union of the lily-livered and respectable; and as such to the general public its affairs are of as little interest (or even less, owing to what seem to be its dreary qualifications for membership) as would be those of a trades-union of boilermakers. The only times that outside interest is aroused is when there are squabbles within the union of a faintly ludicrous nature: disagreements between 'high' and 'low' factions which are observed with the same amusement as are those, in the parallel with boilermakers, about who should drill rivets through iron and who through wood. These squabbles cause passionate feelings among the participants, but to outsiders bring the whole institution into contempt.

It is the tragedy not only of the church but of the whole life of the country that this divorce from popular consciousness should occur and continue in an age when for the first time this century there is a demand for religious thinking and religious understanding from the younger generation. For fifty years to experience life religiously was as unfashionable amongst people of intelligence as to put an aspidistra in one's window. Now, after the war and the hydrogen bomb and experiments with extreme forms of atheistic socialism, it is not. This fact says nothing about the merits of the younger generation nor about the validity of religion: but the failure to do anything about it does say something about the church.

People haven't got religion and want it. They are looking round – asking – and they find the church's answer either not worth listening to or unintelligible. Why?

Much has been written recently by Christians on the failure of communication. We have been told we must brighten up our ideas, use modern techniques, sell Christianity like a detergent. In parishes and in missions stages are erected in churches and while the bell-ringer works the tape the young person's fellowship does amateur dramatics. This sort of effort has a certain short-term effect depending on novelty and enjoyment; but when it is over few echoes remain in the audience's heart.

There is the problem of language. It is true that the language that Christians normally use about their beliefs was formed at a time when people's minds worked differently from the way they work now. Once phrases used in the Bible and Prayer Book were readily acceptable: now they often seem meaningless or contradictory. To spend an hour in a church bookshop is as depressing an experience for a believer as for a non-believer: there are millions and millions of words all written with care and devotion and nearly all are useless except to someone in the same condition or of the same character as the writer. They are Holy Noises – like the baa-ing of sheep. They mean nothing to goats nor to other created beings.

The problem of language is a real one, but it is not to be solved by inventing new jargons which will give rise to the same difficulties only in an even less appealing form. What matters is what language is trying to express. The problem of communication can only be solved after the deeper causes of failure have been faced.

Everyone who has had anything to do with attempting to impress or even make much contact with non-believers knows that words are not the most important means; that a gift of the gab has never moved mountains. What is required is a personal effort at sanctity and some sacrifice. And this must be true of a church as of a person. Sacrifice is something that is experienced, felt, by those who come in contact with it: it is the impression that an effort is being made for self-seeking to be given up. In its presence a stranger finds himself acting differently, believing differently, from the way he did before. It can result in a state of grace, in a faith that can move mountains. How often is this felt when in contact with the church?

Christians believe that if a person, an individual, is lacking in grace then he has to do something about it. The first thing he has to do is to repent. This involves him in (1) examining himself for what he has done wrong in the past; (2) making reparations for these wrongs in the present and intending to do better in the future. If he does all this, he is given absolution. If he doesn't, he isn't.

If the church were a person – which it claims in a sense it is – it is to be wondered if it could be given absolution because in spite of all its good intentions for the future it never seems to admit it has done any wrong in the past, nor is in anything but a venerable condition in the present. Or if it does admit this, it does not experience it with contrition. For the church to repent, its imagination of its past would have to include a sense of agony that it inflicted on others.

The world's view of the Christian sense of 'sin' is that it is something that Christians are obsessed by and cannot shake off: whereas in truth it is the opposite. Sin is something that Christians must get rid of; and they believe that they are people who can get rid of the haunting by it. It is those who won't admit that it exists, who already imagine that there is nothing wrong with them, who are either depressed or frantic. Those who do admit it, and make efforts to get rid of it, are distinguished by the clarity of their thinking, the liberation of their energy, and the liveliness of their mind and heart and consciousness. It is a dose of this, and not of gloom, that church people so urgently require. They require it individually, in their hearts; and in some sense communally, so that their efforts may be effective. The pious must give up their selfish exclusiveness, and the impious their self-indulgent lack of courage.

To be in a state of grace is a state of mind and heart; not a force which will be effective like magical powers. What I am trying to say is not that sacrifice and repentance are a guarantee that we can move mountains and make sin disappear, but rather that they are a necessary condition and in fact the only condition by which mountains will be moved for us. What we are told to do is to keep the faith and to try to remain in a state of grace: if we do, the rest may be done for us. We are not supposed to be able to do it ourselves; that was what the Holy Spirit was made available for. We are asked to trust, and to do what we can, and what may be difficult; and then God's spirit will be operative.

We have got to love ourselves and hate the evil that we do. One is not possible without the other. It is this sort of language that we have got to understand, and act on. Does anyone believe that this is possible with only good intentions? The whole point of this argument is to show that it is this sort of language that we should be using and acting on, but that the attempt is impossible and indeed unintelligible, owing to its superhuman nature, without grace.

There is a huge area of this sort of paradoxical way of seeing things that is hardly touched on by modern apologetics; or if it is, then it is dealt with so apologetically that the writer seems to fear he is making a fool of himself and transmits his embarrassment to the reader. This is a pity, and unnecessary, since the whole of the New Testament seems to talk about desire and will, and the proper relationship between God and mankind, in this paradoxical way, and for a Christian to talk on these subjects in any other way would seem to be useless. Loving enemies – losing your life to save it – joy through tribulation – individual responsibility and helplessness – nearly every concept at the heart of the Gospels is described in such terms, which to someone who can think only logically are contradictory, but which to a Christian must make sense. And if the sense that they make is not logical, then it must be more important than logic, and must be treated accordingly.

It is this way of seeing things and this sort of language which, if the church faced up to its responsibilities towards itself and the world, would become natural to it and not a matter of embarrassment. There would no longer be the sneaking fear that it is pretentious to talk about paradoxes; that it is necessary to compromise with custom to have effect. It would be realised that it is because of the church's compromise with custom that it now does *not* have effect. Then there would be possible a new hope of communication.

What is required is a new attitude, and a new way of talking about such an attitude, in the church's *consciousness*. We have got to have new eyes, new ears, and a new ordering of what we hear and see. This attitude we have got to admit is superhuman. We have got not only to understand but to *live* in a state of being wholly responsible and yet not responsible, loving persons and yet fighting what they do, keeping clear of sin and yet knowing that we can't help sinning, caring passionately about our failures and yet not worrying about them at all. We have got to understand and live this attitude so well that when non-Christians say we are crazy we can be both concerned and unconcerned at this opinion, and know that it is both inevitable that they should hold it and yet imperative that we should change their minds. We've got to suffer for the sufferings of others and make this compassion evident, and yet be joyful for suffering having been defeated and try to transmit this joy. We have got to be confident we can do this although it is superhuman, for the reason that the superhuman is what the human is given to do. It then won't matter if this sort of language is on the surface incomprehensible, because it will be more than a language – a way of life. It will be a way similar to that which was the only one ever to make anything comprehensible: and we can't hope to communicate or to do any better than that.

Prism, 1958

The Christian and the Bomb

There is nothing immoral in power, only in the misuse of it. Power is necessary for the peaceful ordering of life on earth. We are entering an age of enormous scientific power quite apart from the question of the H-bomb; and it is necessary that we do, for it is our only chance of alleviating suffering and misery on this overcrowded planet. Any use of such power may go wrong – in the realms of biology and psychology as well as of physics. But the possibility of the use of power may go right: the very existence of the Bomb, without the use of it, may be the one power that is even now saving millions from napalm bombing, chemical warfare, and the spread of 'conventional' battles. This power of non-use does not depend on a trick; it is within the nature of the handling of power.

The most serious argument about the immorality of this position is that it will result in a world in which 'man will live perpetually sundered from man by fear'. But this begs the question. There is a kind of fear that does sunder man from man, and there is a kind that has always, in both secular and religious history, brought mankind together. It is at least possible that fear of the H-bomb will be of the latter kind – and Christians should understand this. They are told that fear of the Lord is the beginning of wisdom; and the Old Testament Lord was not averse to threats of annihilation. And it is in fact striking how little panic there is in face of the Bomb. The quality of the fear is something to be judged within the situation – upon the particular evidence.

The whole question has to be judged like this. There is no principle to guide Christians. The New Testament gives no help about such political choices as between peace and war, order and freedom, means and ends. It talks about the encounter of the individual with God; and was written at a time when few Christians did or could have temporal power, and thus were not faced with large-scale temporal responsibilities. But it is of the very nature of religion that we should not be

165

instructed in this way. What Christians are given clear instructions about is how to try to get to know God's will and to have the courage to do it. The world is the circumstance within which this attempt is made – from which God's will is learned and upon which it is practised. For the Christian, the large-scale choice is of the same nature as the small-scale – a matter of getting to know what God wants from us as persons – an attempt at objectivity within the directly experienced situation. Different persons may understand their tasks differently. Out of the efforts of each person to understand his own task truly will come the pattern by which the whole is ordered.

Prism, 1958

Mohammed and Monotheism

The Koran does not have much mythology of its own. The most frequent stories, often repeated, are of Moses and the bulrushes, Moses and the rod which turned into a serpent, Noah and the flood, and the call to Abraham. There are even – also repeated – the stories of Zacharias and Elisabeth and of the announcement of a birth to Mary. But here the parallel with the Bible ends. For one of the aims of the Koran is to say just this – the negative purpose of the Koran is to say just this – that this is in fact where the relevance of the Bible ends and nothing else is of importance till the call came to Mohammed six hundred years later. This call told him to declare that he is the one true prophet, that God did not have a son, there was no such thing as an Incarnation, that the complexity or multiplicity of God in the Holy Trinity is a blasphemy. I had thought that the Moslem credo 'Allah is one' was a cry against pagan polytheism, but it seems specifically a cry against Christians – whom Moslems do indeed look upon as polytheists.

Wherever I have travelled in Moslem countries and have had conversations about religion (you can talk to most Moslems about religion; they are confident and fluent) they have said the same thing – that Christians are hypocrites. Moslems know what they believe about God and live it: Christians don't. They either don't know what they believe (try getting a Christian to explain the Trinity!) or they certainly don't practise it. I have had this conversation with Moslem students even when we have been drinking wine together, which is forbidden by their religion.

There was a time when I admitted such accusations against Christians sadly; I sometimes thought it proper to qualify it. But the other day it struck me that one should perhaps even admit it cheerfully – that this accusation is at the crux of difference between Christians and Moslems.

I tried to say (in Morocco, at night, in broken French, on the edge of a cobbled street of donkeys carrying cedar-wood) that in a sense

167

Christians were inevitably hypocrites because this was what their faith accepted and indeed involved them in; it made complex demands on them that they could not always fulfil, and so to outsiders it must always seem that they practised something different to their preaching. But it was their acknowledgement of this that for them made everything all right: because in fact it is a universal human predicament seldom to be able to practise exactly what you preach, and the important question is whether or not you recognise this. And Christians, by the recognition of their 'fallen' nature and of the efficacy of the 'repentance' implied by just this recognition, were given a faith and possibly a grace through which things were done for them which they failed to do themselves. And because Christians were the only people who saw this as the true situation, they were in a sense the only people involved in a religious struggle at all. Others, determined to stick to simple codes of rules and imagining that this was what God required of them, and even that they were succeeding, were putting themselves outside effective human responsibility.

Of course none of this got through. It is an odd fact that hardly any Christian converts are made from Mohammedanism. Apart from the Trinity, the piece of Christian dogma that outrages Moslems is the Incarnation. What an abasement, they say, for God to have a son! and for this God to be crucified! God is one and almighty: God does not need a son.

But it is the point of the Christian story – of God having a Son and allowing this Son to be on earth and to be crucified – that God is showing that he has chosen in most respects to be powerless on earth except through the agency of humans. He has given humans instructions and examples concerning power; and then freedom to act as they choose and to bear the consequences. It is through a realisation of this gift however that they can exercise power truly.

Prism, 1962

The Old Testament and
Paradise Lost

An author hopes that a reader will read his book straight through, because this is the best way to understand it. Some months ago I set out to read the Bible straight through, instead of in small bits which Christians traditionally are accustomed to do. It is true that one gets a new idea of the Old Testament this way: there is very strongly the sense of time, of history; also of the way in which (as in all good books) the changing patterns of the story affect the reactions of the reader. The achievement of Moses – stretching through Exodus, Leviticus, Numbers Deuteronomy – appears enormous. The story of David is a beautiful oasis in a desert of kings (the narrative technique of the books of Samuel, with all except essentials left out, should be a model for any novelist). The book of Job, coming after the flatlands of Ezra, Nehemiah, Esther, is one of the most mountainous and disturbing poems in the world. Towards the end of the Old Testament however, after hundreds of pages of angry or ecstatic prophets, the reader feels a weariness such as the Jews must have felt after so many centuries of chaos and savagery. I think this last point is important. The final effect of reading the Old Testament straight through is an exhausted longing for the light and stillness of the Gospels.

The story of the Old Testament on its own is a story of failure; without the New, it ends in darkness. It is the story of man's ideas about God, not God's story of himself: and man's ideas about God were always going wrong – even the ideas of the greatest prophets. The prophets told of a God who flew into rages, took vengeance, hounded nations and persons with destruction – and this seems to me to be 'wrong' in the light not only of the New Testament but in the light of what most Christians believe. Nowadays when Christians are asked abut what they think of these awkward passages in the Old Testament they say something like 'of course this is not the literal truth, it is a way of putting it according to man's incomplete understanding at the time'. But they are chary of using the word 'wrong'. It is difficult, I suppose, to use this word about what we also call 'holy writ' or the 'Word of God': and I don't suppose it matters to many Christians what word they use, since they know what they mean by 'poetic truth', and have an experience of God stronger than such semantics.

But still, there is something strange in our custom of reading out at Morning and Evening Prayer passages which, as Bishop Gore said, represent 'an incomplete and therefor defective moral and spiritual enlightenment'. It is likely, surely, that these passages might have a defective moral and spiritual effect upon some people who hear them – if not upon the saintly or learned, at least upon the multitude of muddled thinkers and certainly, one would suppose, upon those who come to the Bible or to church in ignorance or inquiry. We call the Bible 'the book of the Church' and we say, when pressed, that only the instructed can interpret it. But we don't treat it like an esoteric document; nor is our instruction about it clear except to those who are so sophisticated in the faith that they don't need it anyway.

I was made to think of all this by a new book by William Empson called *Milton's God*. Professor Empson is a poet, professor and teacher; and his book contains a savage attack on what he takes to be Christianity. He directs his attack mainly at the God of *Paradise Lost:* but he claims (with reason) that Milton took his God from a reading of the Bible, the early fathers, the reformers, and traditional theology. Empson appears well-read in all these sources, and in his last chapter he states his objections to Christianity as a whole –

> The traditional God of Christianity is very wicked . . . A parent who foresaw that his children would fall and then insisted on exposing them to the temptation in view would be considered neurotic, if nothing worse . . . but if he is going to send nearly all of them to hell as a result of Adam's fall . . . this God seems to be wickeder than any recorded society . . . Terms such as 'redemption' are metaphors drawn from the slave-market. It is hard to call up the identity of Father and Son at such points, and envisage God as driving a hard money-bargain with himself before he agrees to torture himself to death out of love for mankind. And yet, as soon as we let slip the veil of identities . . . the only intelligible motive for him is a sadistic one . . . Only if this God had a craving to torture his Son could the Son bargain with him about it. In return for those three hours of ecstasy, the Father would give up the pleasure of torturing for all eternity a small proportion of mankind. Though such a tiny proportion, it has usually been agreed that his eternal pleasure can scarcely be diminished.

I have quoted all this because it is unlikely that many readers of the *Quarterly Review* will read Professor Empson's book, and indeed unlikely that they come across much of this sort of virulence elsewhere. But I think it important that Christians should face this sort of attack, because only by this can they realise the kind of impression some clever atheists get from Christian documents.

Readers of the *Review* will, I suppose, know how to answer it. They will say that Professor Empson has misunderstood the whole story from A to Z – from the creation of humans with free will to Atonement. But what they might find harder to answer is the claim that this misunderstanding is in some sense a reasonable one from the face value of much Christian writing. I think myself there is something in this claim, perhaps because I once felt somewhat like Professor Empson.

It is true that the God of the Old Testament is plainly said to be the active agent of punishment and destruction: it is God himself who turns Adam and Eve out of Eden and multiplies their sorrow; it is God who sends floods, plagues, earthquakes, fire, suffering, upon those who disobey him; who lets Job be tormented and his entire family killed for a bet; for whom sacrifice often seems the only way of satisfying his anger. If you ask most sensible Christians what they think of this, they will probably say – 'It's not God who punishes sin, it is man who by sin cuts himself off from God and thus brings suffering upon himself; suffering is in the world anyway, and by cutting himself off from God man becomes helpless in front of it'. Likewise they would say that God sends no one to hell, but that people seem capable of getting themselves into a position that might be called hellish; though no one still has a right to suggest that, with God's mercy, anyone is likely to remain in such a state. The whole emphasis in speaking of this kind of thing is on man's freedom – the free will which was given him by God when created – by which he can turn himself towards either destruction or salvation, and by which he can make his sufferings either intolerable or not of primary importance. God inflicts suffering on no one, such Christians would say: man inflicts suffering on himself and on his neighbours; just as he did at the incarnation upon God. God is that by which is made possible both freedom and the chance of salvation – for an individual and for the world.

But if this is what we believe about God, then what do we say about the quite different language of the Old Testament? If we are anxious (as I think we should be) about learned men like Professor Empson's total misunderstanding, should we not say unequivocally that the Old Testament in some obvious sense is just 'wrong' – as well as some other cherished Christian documents? The reason why we are chary of so doing is that we fear that we will thus totally invalidate them. But I do not think this is a true way of looking at validity. The Old Testament would lose nothing if people were more outspoken about it being the awe-inspiring story of the tragedies, follies and straight-forward errors of mankind in their search for God and their struggle to understand Him – as well as of the triumphs and glories. And then I think it could be seen as a unique and triumphant work of art, and could work as art should do, transformingly. Art is not logical: there are 'wrong' things depicted in comedy or tragedy: these add to, rather than subtract from, the truth and validity of the whole. Art can cryst-allise the way in which, so mysteriously in life, good can come out of evil. It is only when art, or life, is treated as being necessarily logical that it becomes barren.

Professor Empson writes at the end of his book – 'I see no hope for Christians until they renounce the Devil and all his works; that is, stop worshipping a God who is satisfied by torture, and confess in public that they have done so'. Well, this is easy: but I think we should do more. I think we should confess our sorrow about the many Christians in the past who had presumably thought in something of the way that Professor Empson describes, and have behaved as if they did. And then we should get on with behaving differently: what else is the point of confession and absolution?

Quarterly Review of the Community of the Resurrection, 1962

The Uses of Adversity

After my book *The Life of Raymond Raynes* was published there were people who said – 'But you are trying to say both that this was a holy man, through whom God worked extremely, and also that he had certain limitations and even faults. You are saying both that his life followed a profound Christian pattern, and yet there were tensions and even sadnesses around it. How can these things be?'

Well, how can they not be?

When we read the Gospels nowadays, what do we make of the story? How do we explain that for 90 per cent of the time the apostles were quite bone-headed about what was going on; that at the crucifixion they ran away, the whole lot, and at least one denied ever having known Christ? And yet it was these people, and especially the one who had denied Him, whom God took over, and through whom the story of the resurrection began to be spread over the world.

And it never seems to have occurred to these apostles – the founders and fathers of the early Church – that there was anything odd in this history, let alone shameful. They were happy to let the Gospels be written about how obtuse they had been. St Peter, presumably, did not try to prevent the incident of his denial being published. And afterwards, as the Church grew, other Christians adopted this attitude: St Paul did not cover up the fact that he had persecuted Christians; nor that he was always liable, but for the grace of God, to make an ass of himself again. He seems even to have gone out of his way to stress this – though in an unemotional and business-like manner.

I think the apostles and St Paul took the attitude that their own prestige did not matter because they were so tremendously conscious that what mattered was being worked out under God. And they knew, which is what nowadays we seem to have stopped knowing, that God on earth works through people – through people being honest with themselves and not trying to keep the truth out.

Suppose for a moment that the apostles had cared about their prestige. Suppose that St Peter had refused to give the *imprimatur* to the story of his denial (in the interests of Church order and decency) or that St Paul had covered up his past and present difficulties (so that his 'image' might be more charismatic). Then we might have had no Church at all. We might have had an interesting sect of St Peter for a few years; a rather hair-raising one of St Paul. But no Church of God, because there would have been no truth; no Spirit through Whom, in this latter age, God works.

If a Christian cares about his own prestige he does so inevitably at the cost of God's. The world and the people in it are observably in a mess; and it is either mankind that is the cause of this or else (one comes to believe) God. It is striking how many so-called Christians do seem to blame God for misfortune and strain. They think that God has let them down. But they can only think that God has let them down if they imagine (as Job did for a time) that they are more important than God.

With the people who do not think their prestige matters but who allow whatever is there to work through them – with these people God can work through their failures and calamities as well as their successes. Often, in fact, God can work through failures just as well as through successes because it is through facing failures that one is more likely to learn. So in this mode of seeing things it becomes doubtful if 'failure' has any meaning.

Thus around the life even of a holy man there may well be tensions and suffering just as within him there may be faults. There may even be more obvious tensions around him than around the lives of ordinary people, because he may be an agent of change in the imperfect world.

Prism, 1962

Prayer

Like most people I suppose newly involved with the Church, I was taught that prayer was something that you did rather than you liked doing; something to do with a Rule of Life.

My Rule of Life involved for a time, amongst other things, saying a psalm morning and evening and catching up with myself whenever I missed, like the omnibus edition of *Mrs. Dale's Diary*. This I often found dispiriting, but imagined there might be some merit in its being a bit grim.

But another part of my Rule of Life was to read the Bible. My efforts to do this haphazardly failed even more often, I think, than my prayers – until I thought I should try to read the Bible straight through, which is what a reader should do with any book. So I began again at Genesis and went on and on and on; and then I did get interested in the story. During the time (centuries it seemed) that it took me to get through the Old Testament, my experience with my Rule and the story that I was reading seemed all much of a piece, since the Old Testament was mainly to do with a perpetual and eventually hopeless struggle with something called the Law. But then I came to the New Testament and it seemed like an entirely new book.

In particular, I had only been reading a few days when I came across – 'In your prayers, do not go babbling on like the heathen . . .'

This was in the New English Bible. I checked it with the authorised version: 'When ye pray, use not vain repetitions.' But then, had not the Church been using repetitions for centuries? And were they surprised if they sometimes seemed vain?

And if anyone was now going babbling on, morning and evening, was it not me?

The more I read of the New Testament, in whatever translation, the more it seemed to me that this was at the back of what nearly all the writers were saying – that in the old days, or in some infancy of religion, there was something called Law or Rule of Life which in some form or other involved what might be called babbling; but when a person grew up, he was expected to emerge into some dispensation to listen and think for himself. This did not exactly cancel out the Rule of Law, which was still there and which should be given due respect and reverence. But it seemed plainly to demand that as an adult, one should try primarily to pay attention to the Spirit.

So it seemed to me that the New Testament was telling one to pray when one felt it right to, or wanted to, or needed to; and when one did pray one should not often take much longer than the Lord's Prayer takes (fifteen seconds at my speed). Anything much more, or more elaborate, would be on the threshold of babbling.

So now when I pray I try to have in mind what's been up with me, with the world, with anyone I know – and I say, in not too many words, 'Thanks' or 'Sorry'. And for the rest, at grim moments during night or even the day when one needs a mantra running through one's head to banish devils, I intone – Lord have mercy – and at such times this does not seem like a babble.

Prism, 1962

Freedom Made Available
by God

At the moment Anglicans are confused in their ideas about God. This seems to me not all that bad a situation, because He is by definition indefinable, and people who imagine they are clear about God are usually seeing only their compulsions and projections.

From the beginning Christians have recognised that it is easier to talk about what God is not rather than about what He is; also that it is possible to hint at what God is through the use of images. The reason why Christians want to talk about God at all is because they have an experience of Him; but this does not make it easy to talk. The Christian images of God are in no sense definitions (early attempts at definition were mostly concerned with what God was not) but are attempts to grasp by poetry and art what is inexpressible by reason. Poetry is a use of words which in its effects is personal: that is, poems may properly mean some things to some people and other things to others. Poetry is not wholly subjective because there is in time a common recognition of what is true poetry and what is not: but there are always some who see nothing in poetry at all.

It is thus with Anglicans' ideas of God. Their experiences of God are to some extent common – to do with that which seems to be all powerful, and yet to leave free; which cares, yet enables humans to be responsible for themselves. These paradoxes make it likely that Christians will see God in different ways.

There are still Anglicans I'm told (though I've never met them) who think that God is literally an old man in the sky, who interferes and occasionally casts thunderbolts. This image of God is akin to that of ancient Greeks.

There are other Anglicans, more sophisticated, who know well that God is not an old man in the sky, but because it is difficult to envisage just what He then is, continue to imagine Him for practical purposes as something like an old man in the sky – for purposes of prayer and worship, that is. These Anglicans are sophisticated because this can be a valid use of imagery, arising from the need to formulate in some way what otherwise cannot be envisaged. Thus an Anglican who prays 'as if' to an old man in the sky while knowing well that what he prays to is not an old man in the sky, is not being naive or hypocritical but, simply, human. It seems to be the human predicament that certain profound requirements are only thus able to be honoured; and it is the man who denies this who is naive. The honouring of 'as if' can lead to more complex formulations and states of consciousness.

The important aspect of the 'as if' state of mind is that one should be able to bear the burden of its complexity and not slip into the extremes of either thinking that God is really an old man, or that because He is not an old man one cannot pray or there is nothing to pray to. Either of these extremes is easier; the virtue of complexity is that one can learn.

There are other Anglicans who see the force of the above position but who, because of their cast of mind, do not need or want to see God in any personalised imagery, but who still wish to find representations by which to speak of Him. There is a fashionable phrase now (1965), amongst Anglicans which describes God as 'the ground of our being'. This appeals to people who are too pernickety to accept a personal image but perhaps blunt enough to welcome an abstract one.

It seems to me that the people who are dealing properly nowadays with this search in words for new imagery are the poets who write, simply, poetry. Poets who nowadays write about God do not seem to be writing directly about God: their imagery is of the created world, of the wonder of man's experience of it; and it is through this that they give some hint of the wonder that is God. The best known modern example of this sort of writing is Eliot's *Four Quartets*, which is indeed about God and man's experience of God, but it is the totality of the imagery that gives an idea of God, and not a single image here or there.

Then there are the painstaking and progressive Anglicans who have almost given up talking about God so obscure is the linguistic problem and so impossible the requirements of preaching about it. These people say – All right, the old images have become corrupted and there is too much misunderstanding; but this does not matter, because we can still be good Christians without talking about God, since we have before us the example of Christ. This knowledge of Christ is before us in the Gospels, and this is an example we can follow and can commit ourselves to. We do not need more than this because Christ has told us that through Him is our knowledge of the Father.

These people get on with the job of being Christians – they run lively churches, write encouraging books. But there is some anomaly in their position because although they suggest that God need not be talked about, yet their authority for extolling the person of Christ must rest on something other than their own impressions of Him. If it does not, they are in danger of picking what they want from his multifarious examples according to their own predilections.

The most likely people nowadays, it seems to me, to demonstrate a lively idea of God are those who take nothing on trust, accept nothing blindly, but who observe and learn through their own experience and then find that here there are intimations of divinity. These arise from the experiences, if truly faced and struggled with, concerning the most important happenings in our lives – those in which we love, marry, work, commit ourselves; fail, endure, succeed, bring up children. There is some sort of patterning, interplay, in these areas in which we do not progress logically or in a straight line as it were – choosing our ends and then working out the means for attaining them – but rather that we have a chance to learn from experience a certain style, a certain means of doing things, and then the ends will look after themselves. If we try directly to impose meaning in these areas we fail; but if we have an idea about how to trust, how to have faith quite apart from the aims and assessments of results, then it is possible that we do not fail. Also, we find meaning. It is in this faith and experience that there lies the true idea of God.

It is fundamentally the question of ends and means. The person with no idea of God has to force himself to try to plan for ends. The man who does have an idea of God trusts that if he learns and honours proper means then God will look after ends. This trust is not only a result of his idea of God, but also, because it seems to work, the sustaining cause of it. It is a two-way process. What first gives one the idea of God is likely to be both some outer propulsion, and some decision to jump in the dark.

This begs the question of what is the 'style' of this way of doing things. But it is the attempt to answer this that is the business of religion. In Christianity the means are not laid down in a set of rules; they are described in stories, parables, poems, that are often paradoxical. The image of Christ with which we are confronted in the Bible does not tell us exactly what to do, it tells us the kind of person to aim to be. But the reason we trust this image of Christ – why we talk about Christ's divinity – is because we find we can learn how this can be done, and that it is effective even if often felt to be on a knife-edge. The fact that by trusting the images provided by Christ, and by trying to do something to live in the style of them, events and experiences do occur which offer meaning to our lives and which otherwise would not seem possible – this is evidence for something that might be called divinity: something working beyond ourselves, in and through the world, for our own (and perhaps the world's) proper functioning and health.

Without an idea of a God that holds possibilities open it is difficult to have an idea of freedom that works: man is either machinery which is compelled, or he is flailing in a void. With the idea of a God which holds choices available, humans have freedom to choose; but they will be choosing means and not ends. Ends are the result of a totality of choosings, and are in the province of God.

20th Century, 1965

Philip Pullman's Theology

Philip Pullman's *His Dark Materials* trilogy is a gigantic adventure story in which two children, eleven-year-old Lyra and twelve-year-old Will, find themselves destined to rescue humanity from the confusion and helplessness under which it has laboured ever since its evolution from apes.

The story moves between different worlds. The children themselves come from different worlds; they have to fight with, or are befriended by, angels, witches, spectres, harpies, bears. The idea of alternative worlds comes from a conjecture proposed by physicists to explain the mysteries of quantum mechanics.

In *His Dark Materials* the basic stuff of the universe is called Dust, which is the equivalent of what physicists call Dark Matter. Modern physicists have found it necessary to believe in the existence of all-pervasive but invisible Dark Matter as an explanation of what holds the universe together and prevents it from flying apart through forces of gravity. In *His Dark Materials* Dust is ubiquitous particles of con-sciousness from which everything emanates – matter, mind, life, God, angels, devils. God is the first angel; but he has delegated power on earth to a ruthless angel Melatron, who demands subservience and obedience from humans in the manner of the Old Testament God. In the Bible story Adam and Eve disobey God's instructions, wishing to learn for themselves knowledge of good and evil. God calls this disobedience and sin, and punishes Adam and Eve by turning them out of the comfortable but mindless Garden of Eden and telling them that humans will now have to work and sweat for their livelihood and suffer pain.

The equivalent of this in the *His Dark Materials* story is the decisive step in evolution that took place some 30,000 years ago, when Dust concentrated its attention on humans and they became conscious of its effects. The equivalent in the scientific story is the moment when the first self-conscious human evolved from a chimpanzee some

40-30,000 years ago – as a result of a chance mutation in the brain in conjunction with a condition in the environment of which the newfound consciousness could take advantage.

In all three accounts however some sort of curse remains. Humans are not free or at ease with their consciousness; their desire for knowledge had landed them with guilt, fear, enmity, anxiety, resentment. Many prefer still to place themselves under the orders of an Authority – a Church, a God – which can be held responsible, rather than to accept responsibility for the world themselves.

In both the *His Dark Materials* story and the Bible story a second opportunity for cosmic choice is required, by which humans will have the chance neither to be slavishly obedient nor to feel self-laceratingly at odds with themselves, but to feel free to work with diligence in partnership with other conscious entities in the universe (including matter) to maintain this autonomy and to go where it will take them.

It is here that the *His Dark Materials* story and the Bible story diverge.

In *His Dark Materials* the 'second Eve', who is required so that humans can make a choice for true freedom, takes the form of the young girl Lyra; who by her own courage, canniness, trust, perseverance, will be able to get to the point where the crucial choice is presented to her, and she will have the chance of choosing what is right. If she does this, then her choice will, by its nature and circumstance, enable humans to make right choices themselves when chances occur.

Early in the long and immensely complex story it seems that the choice will have to do with humans being freed by a direct assault on the fortress of the Authority, or the so-called Oblation Board, the Church. This assault is being planned by Lyra's father, Lord Asriel, who has assembled an army in a neighbouring world with elaborate weaponry. Lyra's mother, Mrs Coulter, a bewitching *femme fatale*, seems sometimes to be on the side of her husband Asriel and sometimes on that of the Authority. Lyra comes for a time under the spell of each; but they both seem obsessed with power – and so how will their victory result in a rule any different from that of the Authority?

After innumerable vicissitudes and battles and movements between worlds, Lyra and Will go down into the World of the Dead, where ghosts wait helplessly in a prison-like existence. It is after this that Lyra abandons her father and her mother's power-manoeuvres and is confronted by the true situation in which she has to make her choice. She learns that Dust (consciousness) had been leaking into nothingness because there is too much confusion and fighting within and between worlds. If Dust is to be saved, then openings between worlds will have to be closed, and beings will have to return to and remain in their own worlds, and to work each in his or her own way to establish a universe of wisdom and kindness and courage and curiosity – freed from the illusion of a Kingdom of Heaven. If they do this, there will be just enough new Dust created by their conscious efforts for one doorway between worlds to be kept open.

Lyra realises that this doorway can *either* be the opening from the Land of the Dead which she and Will have opened earlier and through which sad ghosts can escape from their prison: they will then be able to mingle freely with all other creative atoms of Dust throughout the universe –

Or – a doorway kept open through which Lyra and Will, whom she had now come to know as her beloved, will be able to visit each other in the future from and in their separate worlds.

Lyra chooses to make an end of the hopelessness of Death, rather than to hold on to her beloved. She and Will glimpse that they may eventually be able to mingle together as atoms in the universe that they have freed to be the inter-connected Republic of Heaven.

Philip Pullman has gone on record as saying that his books are an assault not only on the Church but on the idea of God – and this is evident concerning the God as portrayed in the Old Testament. This God demands subservience and obedience, and ruthlessly punishes transgressors. He is not averse to slaughter and genocide and threats of an eternity in hell if he does not get his way. In human terms he could hardly be a more appalling father. This God is also that of the Christian fundamentalists who say that every word of the Bible is literally the word of God.

There is nothing in *His Dark Materials* about the New Testament, but it is here that there are parallels with the story of Lyra. In Christian theology there is a tradition in which Jesus is said to be 'the second Adam' – that is, one who will not be so much concerned with disobedience or sin as with turning upside down the old concept of sinners. That is – sinners are those whom Jesus comes into the world to save. If a human makes a choice to see this, and follow what it implies, then he or she is on the way to being saved.

Also, towards the end of St John's Gospel there is the account of how Jesus tells his disciples that he must leave them and disappear in order that they may learn to be responsible for themselves: so long as he remains with them, he says, they will feel and act as if under his authority. However once he has gone, he will make available to them the Spirit of Truth, who 'will guide you into all truth: for he shall not speak of himself; but whatsoever he shall hear, that he shall speak: and he will show you things to come' (John 16.13). And this is almost precisely what is being made evident to Lyra and Will as their means of tapping the power of consciousness, Dust, as the provider of truth.

Thus wise and faithful Christians should see themselves as allies with Pullman in the battle against relentless fundamentalists, who pluck irrelevant bits of the Bible out of context to serve themselves, while ignoring the crucial information given by Jesus about the need to watch and listen.

As Lyra and Will go on their way to their final confrontation, the details of their story offer much fascination. In Lyra's world every human had a *daemon,* in the form of an animal or bird or insect, which is their constant companion, never moving far from them and with whom they can converse. A daemon can be seen as the soul or conscience – that part of oneself with whom one can converse when confronted by dilemmas or choices. In Will's world, which is our own, daemons are not visible; but Will comes to recognise that his is inside him. The daemons of children can change their form according to circumstance: for an adult the form of a daemon becomes fixed.

One of the machinations by which the Authority and Asriel and Mrs Coulter hope to gain power is by severing children from their daemons. This is a sort of sacrifice of the innocents by which religious people have imagined they might find favour with God.

The weapons with which the children can fight the forces of power-mongers are, firstly, an instrument called an *alethiometer* or 'symbol reader', by means of which, if one can achieve the right state of mind when using it, one will be informed of truth. The state of mind required is one of being both empty and attentive – like that required for meditation or prayer, or indeed what Jesus recommended for listening to the Holy Spirit. (It is mentioned that Keats also had a description of this – 'capable of being in uncertainties, mysteries, doubts, without any irritable reaching after fact and reason'.) The working of this is possible because both mind and the material world are composed of particles of consciousness.

Secondly, Will acquires a *knife* which can cut through openings into different worlds but which can only be used by someone in the same state of mind as that required for the alethiometer. This knife however is an instrument of power which, after it has done its work, will have to be given up. Will has been granted its power by 'grace' for a special purpose – that of opening and closing doorways between different worlds. From now on, wisdom will have to be worked for by one's own efforts. There is also a *spyglass* by which the hitherto invisible particles of Dust can be seen – both their leaking-away and their stabilisation.

By the end of the story Lyra has consigned to nothingness her powerful father and mother; but growing up in her own world she will continue to have as a companion her daemon Pantalaimon, who is now in his final form of a pine-marten. Will, in his own world, will now be able to look after his mother who is frail and dependent on him, and whom he has had to abandon for so long.

During their last time together, in a neutral world, Lyra and Will came to recognise the exclusiveness of their sexual and possessive love for each other. It is this they have had to give up for the sake of the harmonious working of the Republic of Heaven.

Unpublished, 2004

PART VI
Science, Self, God

From *Journey into the Dark*, IV

What is striking about the physics that emerged during the first half of the twentieth century is not just that the findings were bizarre but that they seemed not fitted to be made sense of in words. Heisenberg's Uncertainty Principle, Bohr's Complementarity Principle, referred to observations of occurrences at a sub-atomic level at which rules of logic, of language, did not seem to apply. It appeared that what occurred at this level depended not on an objective system of cause-and-effect, but upon choice and style of experiment. If an event was to be observed for instance then the light shone on it to make it observable affected what was seen to occur: in the dark, it was implied, things existed in a state of potentiality. As experiments became more complex, then experiences became more difficult to define or to understand: results could be described in mathematical form and occurrences could sometimes be repeated; but explanation did not seem to be relevant to what needed to be understood. During the second half of the century there have been further propositions concerning non-locality, action-at-a-distance, which suggest that although on an intelligible level no form of information can travel faster than light, yet in some other mode of understanding it can be shown that once particles have been together – which particles are said to have been at the beginning of the universe – they in some sense remain in a state of instantaneous connectedness independent of the speed of light – even if they have moved to opposite ends of the universe. But still no information can be passed by such connectedness because any particularisation, as distinct from potentiality, would still be dependent on the speed of light. It is as if what was being conveyed by such understanding was that there was a form of existence, of totality, that was necessarily in the dark; but that one should be aware of this if meaning was to be made of what there was in the light.

Such suggestions defy easy rationality; yet maestros of physics not only accept but guard the unintelligibility jealously. Bohr: 'Anyone who is not shocked by quantum physics has not understood it'. Feynman: 'It is safe to say that no one understands quantum mechanics'. Haldane: 'The universe is not only queerer than we suppose but queerer than we can suppose'. And so on. Such pronouncements do not provide information so much as insist that there are limits to information; yet they recognise that beyond these limits there exists a world of what George Steiner referred to as 'real presences'. A corollary of this indefinability is that it is easy for anyone who so chooses to ignore or to mock what it suggests. Thus most scientists can proceed without too much speculation in their practical and necessary jobs of measuring, testing, making things work; and non-scientists can excuse their often condescending ignorance of science by pointing not only to the boring repetitiveness of much of the practical work but also to the shifting inarticulateness of theoreticians. And so there need not be, either for scientists or for non-scientists, any journeys into the dark; and people can feel justified in the circumscription of their games under the light. But for any discovery beyond the circle of one's prejudices and predilections – there is the challenge of the dark.

Philosophers have always confronted the realisation that what is apprehended as reality is conditioned by our mode of perception. Wittgenstein put it – 'We think we are talking of the outside world whereas in fact we are describing the frames of the spectacles through which we see it'. Games have been played for centuries between 'realists' and 'idealists': the point at issue being – where can 'reality' be said to reside, in the spectacles or in what is seen through them. But such an either/or question need only be asked if it is a game that is required – which maybe it is, if philosophers are to go on talking. But as Wittgenstein well knew, the question of where reality resides is not one to be resolved by talking; understanding will come through attention to experience; through getting on with things, watching and listening. Illumination comes not through analysis, but as a by-product of alertness.

Such a stricture may indeed seem unwelcome to literary people whose job it is after all to use language. But then – has it not always been the vocation of true poets, true novelists, to try to say the unsayable – to say what is in a straightforward way unsayable – that which has to be groped for, felt, found, delivered from the dark? What on earth otherwise are such novelists and poets up to? They feel that there are presences to be summoned by words from just beyond the usual scope of words; that some such magic is not only necessary but possible. They knew this before physicists did.

But now it is physicists that look beyond the edges of fields of play and who say – what we have to understand is not so much the nature of the outside world nor the nature of the spectacles through which we see it: we have to understand the nature of understanding. It will be by this that we will have a chance to be in relationship with the world which in a sense, yes, we may create by understanding: and this indeed may not be able precisely to be expressed in words. It may be something that we have to learn to live in the presence of – as if it were a relationship with something living. Einstein remarked that the most incomprehensible thing about the universe was that it was comprehensible. This is the sort of observation one might make about a loved one.

One reason why players and audiences mostly stick to the limitations of their games under the light – can feel justified in ignoring scientists who come in scratching their heads from the dark – is that what scientists say they have found seems to have no direct relevance to the world under the light; and indeed what is apprehensible in the dark world of potentialities in comparison with what appear to be certainties? You do not need to go into the dark unless you wish to stop playing games – and why should you do that, unless you become aware of some real presence as it were in the dark? But if the most incomprehensible thing about the universe is that it is comprehensible – what an invitation to go exploring! How else to make comprehensible, for instance, anything of oneself?

Scientists and philosophers alike were for a long time distrustful of anything that could be called 'mind': there was no need, in a mechanical world, to suppose that mind, apart from 'brain', exists. Philosophers once talked about mind as a 'ghost in the machine': this could be justified when there seemed to be ghosts or ghostliness everywhere – mind could be incorporated naturally into a world infused by God the Holy Spirit. But when the idea of God died, what justification was there for mind: in a world of machinery, why should mind be any more than a complex functioning of matter? But then, lo and behold, there were suddenly scientists saying that when you get down to the basics of machinery it is as if these are not quite what used to be understood as matter: they were states, occurrences, that could not exactly be located or defined – which was the condition that had earlier led scientists to ignore the idea of 'mind'. So some scientific consideration of the idea became possible. Even if the biological function of mind could not be located in the brain (Descartes had placed it within the pineal gland) it might yet be conjectured to exist as some overall property of the brain – and if this proposition could be made a nonsense of in words, then all right, what could not be made a nonsense of in words;

but was not this a philosophers', rather than a scientists', game? And scientists could say – It may be that there is no rationally scientific way of understanding how materiality can transform into mind but this is no reason to suggest that such transformation, and thus what might be called consciousness, do not exist. And anyway, what is the point of going round and round with words: what is to be discovered: what is experienced?

Recently however there have been new efforts to nominate features in the brain by means of which it might be conjectured that consciousness functions; there are bundles of cells called microtubules that in their activities seem to show characteristics more in tune with quantum activity than with orthodox systems of cause-and-effect. They seem to exchange vibrational signals (so it is said) which explore simultaneously any number of possible or potential patterns of activity rather than contain or deliver specific messages – in the manner of the wave-function of an electron before it becomes a discrete particle? in the manner of the unobservable and unusable network by which it can yet be known that particles are connected? Such strings of cells are in their working largely insulated from the more straightforward operations of the brain; they seem to be connected to these at just those points where potentiality (so it might be conjectured) could be transmuted into this or that particular. It is just how such interaction is effected, some scientists say, that may never be able scientifically to be known; but why should it be? The question of how an electron transmutes from one state to another is said to be beyond the bounds of precise scientific definition. But such flip-overs are known to occur; and scientists do no find it difficult to accept the existence of that which is evident but not straightforwardly explicable. If quantum activity cannot precisely be defined or predicted, and mind cannot precisely be located or defined, then why should not mind be a representation, an effect (even perhaps a cause?) of quantum activity? This is a conjectural rather than a logical step: if it were provable, then it would not be what it is – which is a form of understanding dependent on choice. And if the mode of interaction between materiality and consciousness has to remain a puzzle, then has not consciousness always been intrigued by puzzles?

The virtue of a model of the brain that includes such a quantum mode of activity is that it does seem representative of what is people's common experience – that of consciousness being confronted at most moments by an array of possibilities from which one outcome rather than another may occur: as a result indeed usually of external forces, but often also as a result of at least the impression of a choice having been made. But what effects such choice is not likely to appear as a free will rationally worked out – such an idea can be made a nonsense of – but rather as a combination of rationality and a largely unconscious network of everything that a person has ever done and experienced and been; some functioning of semi-autonomous interconnectedness. And what more can be said about this – except that of course it cannot be proved but seems to be the case. That is – people's lives go on their way not wholly as a result of genetic or environmental conditioning, nor simply as a matter of rational or sentimental choice; but rather in a style resulting from the interactions of all these forces and more – the means by which a person does have some autonomy, perhaps being just that by which he recognises such processes going on; and by this influences them. Myriad and minuscule chances, reactions, choosings make persons what they are; this is what affects further choosings, reactions, chances. The language becomes incantatory; how should it not? This is what is being suggested, found – that any attempt to make language more precise makes that which is particular, yes, but loses what is potential. And more than this – what is being suggested without too much being said (God help us) is that if one is attentive enough to possibilities, to the fact that there is a world of possibili-ties, then the particular that occurs may well happen to seem more right than others might have been; and one will have an experience of rightness as one does with a work of art; and through what other form of understanding might this seem to have occurred?

It was when the idea of God was dying that so was that of 'mind'; and with these deaths also those of the ideas of 'good' and 'evil' – for what could be the validity of these without the acceptance of some transcendental authentication? The reason why the idea of God was dying was because it, along with everything else, was being dragged under arc-lights: there it lay like a stranded whale upon a beach while people chopped at it – to try to see how it worked, to take out their fear, hoping to get food. But things do die when out of their element; that which is numinous lives in the dark. In the course of evolution it seems that impressions had to be dragged into the light of scientific analysis; this is what the human brain had become equipped to do; it was what the environment seemed to demand that the human species should do if it was to survive and flourish. But not everything thrives in the light. It was prelates and theologians who tried to define God, to pin God down, to tell Him what He could and could not do – as if He were their acolyte or a butterfly staked on a table. And God might still be put forward as a patron of science by people who wished to harness Him to their programmes and prestige: in a mechanistic world why should God not be seen as a Prime Mover, First Cause: some power who, more feasibly than upstart Natural Selection, had got numbered every hair for instance on every animal's head – as an almighty taxonomist should. But what a role for God! Perhaps it was simply on account of the dismalness of such a function that the idea of Him died. And then had to wait for resurrection at the hands of people who wished to do what is proper for humans to do in relation to God – which is, watch and listen.

For Christians at least there is a precise story about this however enigmatic – the story of how God seems to disappear, which He said He had to do if people were ever to learn things for themselves: but then if they kept their wits about them they would find Him again, in the sense of being led into all truth. And so, in the course of time, there were indeed those who watched and listened – who were trying to see through to the nature of the universe rather than to force it to fit the frames of their spectacles; experimenters who came upon at the very centre and at the very edges of the universe areas of darkness that contained what had to be called numinous; and so once more started to talk of what was indefinable, unknowable, incomprehensible – in the way that old prophets and mystics had once insisted that God should be talked about. And if scientists wanted a word for that which seemed to exist so totally and centrally but about which one either could not speak or had to recognise that what one said were conjectures and not certainties – well, why not 'God'?

Or perhaps the word had become too tainted to be sensibly used: prelates and theologians had been orating as if God were their captive model; religionists were showing their lantern-slides of God and not welcoming those whose snaps were different. But then – had it not been told how Jesus founded his church on the disciple he knew would deny him? And so – is there not here some cosmic irony; some secret ruse? May there not have to be dogmatic churchmen, proud prelates, that is, so that there will be maintained a formal worldly structure within which, in spite of appearances, there will be preserved and guarded the lore, the imagery, the poetry, the teaching; through the availability of which each person can have the chance to learn, to listen, to go his or her own way? This may properly be the style of earthly structures; how else should the numinous be available to each in his or her or its own way?

The myths and images that arise at the beginning of a civilisation and are then elaborated are the results of the instinct to understand what has burst upon consciousness like armies of paradox, cohorts of the indefinable: how is it, for instance, that a human seems to be both an animal and to have the qualities of a god: both to be helplessly bound by inheritance and circumstance and yet to have the freedom and vision to change the world? Such questions can be formulated by reason but cannot be answered by it; reason likes to come down on one side or another. In myths, images, there can be presented the experience of how in matters of life and understanding opposites can be apprehended as one. A myth is gutted by too much elucidation: it loses its power. If a civilisation loses its relationship with myth it is gutted – it is split by and into opposites and is at enmity with itself. It is possible to retain an awareness of beauty, but beauty depends for its health on the sustenance of myth. If this is taken away, then beauty is left trying to look at itself – and drowns like Narcissus. When you stand in front of a true work of art you are confronted by a represen- tation of wholeness; of the way in which everything is connected to everything else; of the way in which you, through the art-work, are connected to everything else; and what is being understood is the nature of understanding. Sometimes it is difficult to leave a work of art and go on one's way (those watchers held by a last glimpse of the Taj Mahal!) and yet how impossible to remain for ever in the presence of such god-like potentiality! One has to move on to somewhere where one can send messages such as just – How are you? Wish you were here! We are having a wonderful time. And then again move on. But something will have occurred from the having been in the presence of connectedness: one is aware of this; but not quite of what.

A state of grace is one in which you are in the dark: but oh well, yes, you know that light is possibly everywhere in the dark, it is just that it has no object to reflect it. You are in the present: the future you cannot know; you may be haunted by the past; but you can alter its meaning, and even for the future, if you see that you have choices. What one is haunted by are the consequences of one's prejudices and predilections: oh these were pathetic, yes, but so what! they fall away in the dark; there is so much in the present to be attended to. The past can be altered by the present not in itself nor much in its conse- quences but in what one makes of these; a pattern stretches through one between future and past. Prayer once seemed a means of freeing oneself in the present from the past; of having hope and assurance for the future. One was talking to one's self or to one's not-self: what was the difference so long as one listened, one saw there were possibilities. And not only concerning one's own choices. Prayer is the opposite of the fashion of informing God what He should or should not do, what He can or cannot be. In prayer one is not so much talking, as even to one's own voice listening. One prays properly for a state of grace to occur: a state in which there might stop the furious buzzing in one's head – the bees that fly out in search and pursuit of passions and prejudices. Rather, there may be the image of oneself by the bank of a stream and throwing bread upon the waters; and not worrying too much about whether it will come back after many days; some of it will go somewhere. And what a miracle is the light on the water! Is that a rainbow covenant? Are the colours out there or in one's head? What a stupid question to ask of a rainbow! Is it not patently both? And it is beautiful.

Unpublished, 1998

What Price Political Idealism?

My efforts to sympathise with my father, Oswald Mosley, came to grief, as did so many people's, on the rocks of his alliance with anti-Semitism. How could a man of such intelligence and wit in his private life have fallen prey to forces that seemed not only immoral but self-destructive? He was such an idealist! Were there grave dangers, as well as possible virtues, in political idealism?

Oswald Mosley had entered Parliament as the youngest MP in 1918. He had fought in the trenches in the First World War, had been invalided out of the Royal Flying Corps, had been appalled by what he had seen of war's needless horrors. His idealism became set on trying to prevent such a war happening again.

In Parliament he was at first a Conservative, a member of Lloyd George's coalition government ostensibly dedicated to building 'a country fit for heroes to live in'. The government in fact seemed to be preserving the status quo of what were called 'the hard-faced men who had done well out of the war'. It was also using brutal methods to maintain British rule in Ireland. After a few years Mosley left the Conservatives and joined Labour.

The Labour Party was supposedly dedicated to dealing with the problem of the rapidly growing unemployment. In the 1929 Labour government Mosley was made the junior minister responsible for this task. He put forward ambitious neo-Keynesian proposals about how to kick-start the economy by selective injections of government money. His plans were turned down by the Labour hierarchy who followed traditional dogma about the need for balanced budgets.

Along with other idealistic young men of the time my father saw the slump of 1930-31 as heralding the end of democratic capitalism. If Britain were not to collapse into chaos or communism, it seemed to him a new movement had to be formed that would not be shackled by the hidebound timidity of the old parties. He felt himself equal to this task. But for a new political party to get off the ground a more urgent impetus was needed than the call to an idea.

Just at this time, early in 1932, he visited Italy. Here Mussolini had been in power for nine years and had organised around him a country of obvious vitality, even though there were dark stories of the means used to achieve this. But still it could be argued – was not energy in practical terms always achieved at some cost?

Mussolini was soon offering my father money to back a fascist movement in Britain. Such payments would have to be kept secret because the appeal of fascism was to be seen as rigorously nationalistic. My father accepted the offer: was this not the sort of stratagem, doublethink, that most politicians had to swallow? But then – was he not dedicated to breaking away from old political duplicities?

This confusion was the first nail in the coffin of idealism.

In January 1933 Hitler came into power in Germany. Almost immediately it was evident that, firstly, Germany would very soon become the leading fascist power in Europe; and secondly, that at the centre of Nazi idealism was a virulent anti-Semitism.

Up to this time Mussolini had shown few signs of anti-Semitism. In my father's inaugural manifesto for his British Union of Fascists in 1932 there had been no mention of Jews. But now, if there was to be any cohesion amongst European fascists, what accommodation was to be made with Nazi anti-Semitism?

For a while during 1933 my father went his own way. He wrote – 'racial and religious persecutions are alien to the British character'; and – 'Hitler has made his greatest mistake in his attitude to the Jews'. He was even called a 'kosher fascist' by dissident right-wing extremists. But soon he was doing nothing to stop his followers parading through the streets in Nazi style and singing songs to the same tunes as German and Italian fascists: and thus it became inevitable both that convinced anti-Semites were attracted to his banner and that Jews should have good reason to fear and to fight this. In 1934 my father acknowledged he was involved in a battle with Jews: he claimed this had been thrust upon him, but he did not withdraw from it: it seemed that to do so would mean disbanding his whole short-lived movement, and then politically where could he go? He had burned his boats with the old parties. And he could always argue to himself that means might be justified by ends; virulence might calm down if he stayed within the fascist fold. He might even have a restraining influence upon Hitler.

But this acceptance of anti-Semitism was the second and perhaps decisive nail in the coffin of idealism.

There are no excuses, but perhaps a few explanations, for my father's embracing of anti-Semitism. He had never been an orthodox politician. His impatience with the old parties had set him up as a maverick, a one-man band; someone who had no time for the petty machinations of politics. He was an orator, a prophet: he had a wonderful way with words and a trust in their power. He thought that if a policy seemed reasonable then words could be used to implement it; people would follow the force of a logical argument. He seemed to have no vision of the effects that an emotive use of words would have on people.

When he formed his own fascist party this provided him with a platform, but his style did not essentially change: he did not pay much attention to the day-to-day running of his party, nor to the increasingly scurrilous anti-Semitic items that were printed in its newspapers. He left all this to his increasingly prejudiced lieutenants, while he went round the country making his speeches to mesmerised audiences about how to solve all the problems of the world. This made no sense in practical terms with regard to a party intended to demonstrate leadership and discipline. Also his own style of oratory was becoming tainted. But it was as if he had begun to feel in his bones the futility of the political machinery he had allied himself to. There might still however be virtue in the propagation of an idea.

In illustration of this there is the example of the notorious 'Battle of Cable Street', the culmination of the fascists' virulent anti-Jewish campaign in London's East End in 1936. In folk-lore this has gone down as the battle in which local residents fought and routed a fascist march. In fact the battle was between anti-fascists and the police who tried, unsuccessfully, to clear the street of barricades while the fascists, on police orders, stood meekly to one side in their military-style uniforms and eventually, to the jeers of the crowd, turned and went home. This was (and it was seen thus at the time) a far more degrading political defeat for the fascists than would have been any outcome of direct confrontation with the enemy: but such were people's preconceptions of politics that it did not seem possible that my father, known to be physically courageous, could simply have thought that a violent confrontation would not have made sense. But the evidence is that my father, once he realised there was little chance of his message being heard – the plan had been that he would make short speeches at street corners – had seen no point in becoming involved in a squalid brawl: was it not important that fascists should be seen as law-abiding? And as it happened, shortly after this many of his more virulent lieutenants left him – on the grounds of his fading belligerence. And even before this the funding from Mussolini had ceased, and an envoy from Hitler was soon reporting back that

Mosley was less a practical politician than a dreamer.

My father seemed to accept all this with equanimity. Perhaps he would now be able to move with less encumbrance round the country with his Messianic message – There need be no more war! All the problems of the world can, if people listen, rationally be answered!

But what can be done about a father who trusts in the power of such a message?

By the time I was old enough to have any sensible view of my father – in say 1937-38 when I was fourteen – politics did not play much part in what I saw of his life. He would return from his speaking-tours to the beautiful house in Derbyshire where he lived with my stepmother; he would bring no henchmen nor trappings of his politics with him; he would tell his funny stories about old-style politics. He would answer carefully any questions that I put to him about ideas, or what was happening in the world. For the rest, he would take me with him fishing or shooting or occasionally riding – then he would be off again in his ancient Bentley to challenge or to placate whatever dragons roamed in his strange world.

When he was imprisoned as a security risk in 1940 because of his opposition to the Second World War he seemed to accept this fate too with equanimity. He had, after all, done his best with regard to what he cared about – which was to prevent war.

It was when he was in prison that there began my own close relationship with my father. As a young army officer I was allowed to spend the day with him and my stepmother Diana in their two-roomed cell in Holloway. We would talk – still about books, ideas: we were both dabbling in philosophy, and there was not much point now in my pressing him on politics. By the time I returned from the war in Italy he had been released and was living the life of a country gentleman in Wiltshire. I went to stay with him. He said he did not want to go back into politics.

I wanted to be a writer. Our relationship flourished for two years. Then by the time his old followers began enticing my father back into politics at the end of 1947, I had married and was moving to live far away in North Wales. He and I did sometimes now correspond about politics. He had started his own movement again, this time based on a European rather than a British nationalism; but by the mid-1950s this was becoming concentrated on a programme aimed at preventing black immigration. I thought this policy insane – not only on questions of right and wrong (I was in the process of becoming a Christian under the wing of people involved in the anti-apartheid movement), but because he was once more hitching himself to the sort of racist bandwagon that had destroyed his reputation before the war. When I argued with him he went through his rationalisations – his policy was not anti-black, it was that government money should be poured into the West Indies so that blacks would have jobs there and would not want to leave their countries – or if they did, such irrationality would not be the responsibility of the politicians. When I said – This is all theory, words, it has nothing to do with people's actual predicaments – he seemed not to accept the seriousness of such a suggestion. It was as if the power of words had bewitched his ability to look at or to feel about human situations.

I went up, without telling him, to hear one of his street-corner speeches in North Kensington, where black immigrants had settled and where he was standing as a parliamentary candidate for his Union Movement in the 1959 election. And there he was, yes, not only arguing his rational case but now making use of the language of racism – passing on stories he had been told, for instance, of black men keeping teen-age white girls in attics. I felt that the time had come when I had to confront him emotionally, not just rationally; so I bearded him in his campaign office and I told him that he himself, whether consciously or unconsciously, seemed to have been taken over by the rotten racist rubbish that he had for so long duplicitously tolerated in his movements; and if he could not recognise that this was wrong, could he not at least see that it was self-destructive? I had expected a thunderbolt: he just replied quietly – 'I will never speak to you again'. And I had the curious impression that he understood what I was saying, and was sad that I did not see that this was some trap that he felt he could not escape from.

He finally retired from politics in 1966 with by now an almost ineradicable reputation as an anti-Semite and a racist – also a failure. I tried to remember, arising from both his pre-war and his post-war movements, how little violence and brutality there had in fact been in comparison with similar continental movements. Might not after all his talent as a speechifying one-man band have diverted energies from what might otherwise have been more organised fascist horrors? There were considerations here that should make it possible to be on speaking terms again.

By the time he and I had returned to something of our earlier intimacy he was a benign old man nearing eighty and he still loved to talk – and in the old style about books, ideas; also about the past – about the days when I had been a child and my mother had been alive and Hitler had not been heard of. He did also want at least to glance at what might have been 'mistakes' in the more recent past; and he did seem to accept many of these, including his excuses at the time for what he then had not easily seen as Nazi horrors. It was still difficult for him to see how it might not be words, rationalisation, that would alter the world: but by this time I had my own ideas about how things worked – about how one had to watch, and to listen to what turned up, rather than to talk, if one was to be in any useful partnership with how things in the world turned out. I was visiting him a week or so before he died and I was telling him how I thought that in spite of the mistakes and prevarications of the past there was still a pattern from which much could be learned from his life – of both the efforts and the dangers of idealism. And he was watching me and perhaps listening. And then during lunch – this was the last day I spent with him – he announced that when he died he wanted me to have all his papers so that I could write his story.

Sunday Telegraph, 1996

From *Journey into the Dark,* V

So long as it could be imagined that everything might be knowable under the light then dispute and hostility were inevitable: each person's particular vision could be imagined as the whole, and thus feel itself justified in encroaching on and invading others. There was ever less recognition that convictions were framed by the spectacles through which things were seen; that what the world was in itself was intrinsically unknowable except by some odd dispensation. As has been said before – when it had seemed that the outside world was under the authority of God then its unknowability could be accepted in the trust that it was being cared for; though this did not prevent dogmatists claiming that they knew the mind of God. But then when the idea of God died the concept of unknowability seemed to become untenable: what on earth were humans here for except for the outside world to be explored, mapped, colonised? To turn one's back would be to deny the human experience of autonomy. All this made sense – and yet, and yet. The further philosophers went on analysing what might make sense the more they came across what was paradoxical: the further astronomers peered into the universe the more evanescent were boundaries and what might be beginnings; the more physicists delved into matter the more it disappeared and names had to be invented for what might or might not be there. Biologists, more concerned with questions of how things work than of what things are, seemed to be having an easier ride with their cut-throat theories of Darwinian natural selection. But left behind in their wake were unasked questions about how the necessary conditions and components for natural selection got under way; how are these maintained while depending for their functioning on what are called random occurrences. Such metaphysical speculations were held to be outside the realm of science; but they could not quite be banished from the interest of humans. And in this area to be sure there could still be exercised the love of exploration. In fact with the idea of the death of God it seemed that areas of enquiry had been opened up. But if these were beyond the bounds of science, what might give an impression of validity to such exploring?

David Bohm was a physicist who suggested in his later years that thought itself was in some sense the enemy of metaphysical understanding – not just in respect of the limitations of language, but because thought, in working towards answers, was likely to falsify that which was in its nature a range of possibilities. Thought traces the frames of spectacles and claims that it is describing what is seen through them; it loses the recognition that potentiality is the nature of things-in-themselves. Some contact with things-in-themselves is possible if they are conjectured as possibilities: they can seem to exist in some quantum world and it can be supposed that consciousness might make of them this or that. In such a style sense can be made both of consciousness and of the idea of things-in-themselves. The fear and recoil that humans may feel at the lack of objective certainties is the reaction of people whose timidity has not allowed them to experience the adventure of a search – the excitement of which can seem as true as any certainty. It is by looking for how to handle their predicaments that humans may find themselves in contact with reality. But then, if it is not just thought that has helped them, what has? At least thought has got them to recognise the frames of spectacles.

For the style of further exploration David Bohm has suggested that of the artist who, when involved in his work, is aware intensely of himself in the present; of what he is doing but not of where he is going; of the impression that there is something to be discovered by him in partnership with what seems to be waiting to be discovered, even to be putting a hand out to him in the dark. In this way consciousness, being not wholly circumscribed by itself, ceases from being a controlling limitation and can accept that it is involved in discovery – both of what there is in the outside world and of what one might be or be becoming oneself. That such exploration is alarming can be a challenge rather than a deterrent. To realise that oneself, a vestige of the outside world, makes oneself a partner with it by the nature of the experiments one chooses: that one learns what experiments to choose by trying them out on an outside world and upon oneself: that the function of this partnership is to fashion both oneself and the outside world; this is like – what – chancing or accepting the role of another hand as well as one's own in the business of artistic creation; of being aware that what might have seemed at random can give the impression of being correct. With oneself as both the experimenter and that which is being experimented upon – oneself the conjuror and the audience waiting to observe the trick that is after all not a trick but a skill – what a chance for real birds, rabbits, flags, to emerge from a hat!

So long as it seemed reasonable, that is, to suppose that humans were no more than the sum of their parts – genes, cells, molecules or whatever – then indeed it was easy to believe that humans were not responsible either for themselves nor for what went on in the world – in such a condition what could responsibility mean? It was this supposition that offered a person the chance to sink into a comfortable pessimism. But if it can be realised that it is a concatenation of genes and cells and molecules themselves that has discovered, created, through the vast complexity of their conjunctions and interactions, the concept of responsibility – the ability to sort and pick from observed potentialities – then no longer can helpless pessimism seem reasonable; it becomes simply the result of denial. The experience of the availability of choice, that is, has evolved along with everything else; futility is clung to only by those who choose not to look at evidence; who have preferred to see autonomy in anything except themselves; whose infantilism has prevented them from having any aptitude for courage or learning or enquiry. Responsibility is to become aware of innumerable possibilities out of which a particular might become actual by the participation of oneself: what particular occurs has both everything and nothing to do with oneself: one's partnership with the world is to recognise such a choice is there. For the rest, there is indeed what is called chance – both in the presentation of possibilities, and the coincidences by which this or that might become particular. But chance averages out; coincidence is not unusual. And if it is chance that has produced its partner, consciousness, out of presumably almost infinite possibilities, then it is consciousness that can pick and choose from the possibilities provided by its partner chance.

In biology there had grown an awareness of the pervasiveness of death as a necessity for life: in the development of an embryonic form innumerable cells proliferate and a huge proportion have to die; nature does not work by economical design but by the production of surfeits and then the elimination of vast numbers that do not fit into place – 'place' in this context being the result of the selective operation of the environment on genetic replication and occasional mutation. And as with cells, so with seeds, with sperms. This happens to be the most efficient means of shaping what will survive: there are too many imponderables in the environment for efficiency by design to succeed; a component has to find its place by trial and error; and by that which is not suitable being discarded.

This process by which that which healthily lives does so only at the cost of enormous waste is not difficult for humans to accept when look-

ing at seeds, at cells; it is less easy to do so when looking at themselves.
A chance for humans to come to terms with the necessity of death was
provided by the idea of the Selfish Gene. This proposes that humans
are after all not much more than containers; organisms are discarded
like old tin cans; it is the genes that they have contained and that have
fought for survival that can be passed on; that provide the concept of
immortality. This idea was attractive also to those who wish to feel no
more responsibility for growth and fertilisation than that provided by a
seed-packet: but even the most ardent propagandists for the idea hardly
felt this sufficiently explained human experience. Richard Dawkins, the
begetter of the idea of the Selfish Gene, recognised the power of the human individual to have some autonomy concerning what seeds might
be encouraged to live or to die both before and after they are passed on
– by creating the ground on which this or that new phenotype, or human
organism, might flourish. Dawkins has called the units of such potential
ground or culture memes – a word suggesting that in human evolution
such nurturing forces have a status and a function comparable to those
of genes; that by means of technology, art, artefacts, humans do have an
effectiveness in guiding which way evolution will go, by forming and
passing on ideas and formulations that will encourage or discourage what
will survive – even genetically. The individual will die, but will have the
immortality of having influenced that which will not – by means of the
environment that he or she has helped to create. And might this be not
only a compensation for death, but a reason for living?

However arising contemporaneously but far less noticeably than the
idea of the Selfish Gene – less noticed perhaps just because it was not
to do with antagonism and thus less suited to making a splash under
publicists' lights – has been the idea of a process in evolution more
important even than the elimination of one form of life by another;
than the survival of the fit few at the cost of enormous waste. This is
the less spectacular but ultimately more effective process known as
symbiosis – the alliance with, or assimilation of, one form of life by
another; each performing for the other a vital function that it could
not perform for itself. In symbiosis an organism finds that it can best
live and indeed evolve in harmony or conjunction with another; thus
it best serves its own needs and those of the other. The effectiveness
of symbiosis in evolution is that it leads comparatively quickly to a
diversity of forms amongst which nature will have an increased range
of selection. The most persuasive proponent of this idea is Lynn
Margulis who in her book *Microcosmos*, written in conjunction with
her son Dorion Sagan, proposes that the single most important step

at the beginning of evolution was when a single bacterium, up till then the most developed form of life and replicating itself by simple division, happened (how? why? scientists say 'by chance') to invade, to become assimilated within, another such cell, and thus became its nucleus, or some semi-autonomous and potentially genetic component within it. And by this were made available not only the benefits of intricate symbiotic living, but eventually the vastly elaborate systems of sexual reproduction by which mutations might occur and proliferate and become available for natural selection; and thus evolution could go bounding on in ever more complex ways – at least to the point where human conscious occurred which would be capable of trying to understand it. And then, conceivably of guiding it?

What is suggested by glimpses into such unknown areas is that it may be, just might be, what is called consciousness (and this is how conscious-ness might be understood apart from a function of the complexity of matter?) that plays a part in the operation of what is called randomness or chance. In the thought-experiment of Schrödinger's Cat (how often this experiment is trotted out by apologists for paradox! still, does one not have to come to terms with it?) in this experiment a set-up has been arranged in which within a limited time there is a 50-50 chance of a radioactive substance emitting a particle which will break a phial of poison which will kill the cat that is enclosed together with this ap-paratus in a box. Until such a time as when the box is opened and it is seen whether in fact the cat is alive or dead the cat will, according to quantum theory, be neither alive nor dead; it will be in a state as it were of suspended animation. This is because whether or not the radioac-tive particle will have been emitted will not have occurred – nor will not be known to have occurred but will not have occurred – until the occurrence is subjected to some act of observation or measurement; an activity, that is, of consciousness. Until then the condition of the cat remains a possibility, neither one thing nor the other, or both. But then there are the questions – Well what is it, this act of observation or measurement or consciousness that determines the event: why should it not be the cat's observation, after all, that determines whether or not a particle has been emitted; whether or not it, the cat, is alive or dead? Or why should it not be a physicist who is locked up in the box, and would he not be able to tell, until someone looks at him, whether he is alive or dead? The whole situation can be reduced to absurdity – as indeed was the aim of those who originally suggested the experiment, who wanted to discredit quantum theory. But then those who advocated it said – Yes indeed the matter is absurd: but if you like, it is just this you can go on from to search for meaning. There is the alternative, of course, to refuse to look at the evidence.

The reluctance of most literary people to become interested either in everyday science or in arcane scientific speculation is the result not only of timidity: literature, as has been said, for three thousand years has been concerned with confrontation, with conflict, with who will come out on top. The mechanics of everyday science are too painstaking for such dramatics; and speculation moves into areas in which it soon seems uncertain what as it were is bottom and what is top. On literary fringes there have been stories suggesting or involving indeterminacy, complementarity, relativity; but these are usually in the form of science fiction fables, and seem far from usual experience. To be sure a character such as Hamlet spends most of his time on stage in a state of what might be called suspended animation akin to that of Schrödinger's Cat; but it is ordained by the script – and most audiences know this – that he and most of the main characters will end up dead. The appeal of the detective novel or mystery novel may lie in the outcome being uncertain while the search goes on; but there is little appeal in the idea that outcomes might be as uncertain at the end as at the beginning – of satisfaction having been offered by the search. When this is attempted in avant-garde literature it does not command much attention; for there to be excitement in an on-going search there have to be recognisable what are felt as the mainsprings of life. In mainstream literature characters are felt to 'come alive' by virtue of their prejudices and transparent predilections; a character portrayed as being open-minded, to be ready to watch and listen (as good writers themselves surely have to be), is likely to be seen as wishy-washy or even slightly deranged. Relevant to this is the bizarre and widespread insistence that a writer's life has nothing to do with his work. If writers and critics did see their lives in relation to their work, would they not indeed be under some pressure, in the course of the to-and-fro, to question, to change – their lives, their work?

It sometimes seems that children for a time are at home in a world of possibilities: they have to find their own way, what else can they do? At first when children are buffeted or frightened they are likely to see the grown-up world as mad: then when they see the grown-up world has set out a pattern for them they may, in order to survive, have to conform or violently to rebel. In either way the innocence of seeing the grown-up world as simply daft will be lost. Some vestiges of innocence may remain like seeds under snow in winter – to be revived on a young adult's own terms if the chance comes round with the seasons. Indeed it sometimes seems that parents have the chance to recapture some of their own lost innocence from their children; though it is as likely that the children's hurt or accusing eyes will have driven deeper, for a time at least, a parent's envies and resentments: it is rare that a parent learns to watch, to listen.

What is required if one is to feel at home in a journey in the dark (I have said this before? How many seeds does one have to sow before some do not fall on stony ground!) is that, first, it should seem sensible to trust in the co-operation of the darkness with oneself: this is both a prerequisite and a consequence of setting out on a journey. One cannot experience it except originally perhaps by a jump in the dark; then with the experience one may learn that the jump has been worthwhile. But how else would one wish to experience it except through trust – how otherwise can there be wonder? The trust, then with luck the experience, is that what one takes in the dark to be a handrail does not turn out, for instance, to be a snake; or if it does, then what might not a snake be – some hand-hold such as that which helped one to get out of that claustrophobic garden? The state of grace (yes I know one should not keep fussing over what might be taking root) is one in which almost anything can be seen as being right – and so can it become right by being trusted? But try it, trust it. This is what can be said! It is possible there will be hurt: but does one not learn from hurt?

The state of mind required (just wait, then, to see what might be germinating beneath the snow) would be one that could hold, assimilate, complex and even contradictory ideas all at once – those with which we seem to be programmed and those from which we seem to feel some challenge from the dark – not imagining that for the sake of rationality one set has to be sacrificed for the sake of the other, but waiting to see where oneself will be led if they are allowed to interact in their own way. There would be some symbiosis occurring in the ways in which it can be seen that good can sometimes come out of evil though evil can never be recommended for the sake of good; in the ways of seeing the necessity to try to preserve life even it is recognised that life only evolves at the expense of enormous waste: such recognition and such humanity having to co-exist and interact if sense is to be made out of what occurs. Such a state of mind would involve knowing that there are separate and apparently contradictory parts of oneself, but that by knowing this they could effectively be one. Also this one, looking down on oneself, would be something other than oneself – or how, and from where, could it look down? A state of grace (you see! is there not some shoot showing?) is, again, one in which one has the experience of being essentially oneself and essentially part of something other – the one not being possible without the other – and so in essence these are one. This is perhaps the most necessary symbiosis between mind and one's experience of the world – the realisation that one cannot be truly oneself without being part of something greater – in relation to which one is given freedom of movement in a context of pattern. To give expression to such experience has always been difficult; the effort to do so has resulted in religion and religious imagery. There is a need to try to say the unsayable so that humans will be able to see they have a choice; also to glimpse what there might be beyond it. (You thought I might be writing a literary essay? God forbid!)

It is always possible to say that religious imagery is absurd: it usually carries the potency of a challenge. But nowadays there are the small bands of the ostensibly irreligious who march with their flags and banners honouring what is unsayable – the connection and separation between subject and object; a sense of freedom requiring an acceptance of order; a totality represented through results rather than by efforts to describe it. All this may seem more acceptable nowadays than to honour a God both omnipotent and at the same time helpless; at the mercy of autonomous humans whom he has empowered to be self-sufficient. But all these are efforts with words to reach out to what is searched for; never quite possessed. But the message is the same – no not message: what is true cannot be transmitted, only known: you remember? Words are not things in themselves. But poems can be written and images can be carved or painted and these can be things in themselves in that people can confront them and react to them as they choose or like. And they might sometimes find – Oh yes that is exactly right! that is what has been there all the time!

On a raft, on a bit of driftwood, a seed may lodge; may even now have floated to some strange shore – in the mind, I mean, in your mind. Waiting on the land will be the predators who have been programmed to guard the shore – to do battle with any strange creature that is blown their way. But you – you can say to them – Look, you may kill me; you may do what you like: but how does anything survive unless it dies and comes alive again in its own way? Am I talking of myself? I am talking about you! Here is connectedness: let it make of you what you like.

Unpublished, 1998

Stammering

I first became aware that I stammered at the age of about seven. I remembered my mother and my nanny standing over me and suggesting, solicitously, that I try to speak slowly and carefully. Up to this time I had not realised that I did not. I had thought it natural to grope and even stumble for words, in order to find out what one wanted to say.

This was the beginning of a real stammer – the effort to bite back and control words as they came out in something like a burble. Burbling if left to itself usually sorts itself out in time: at some stage in a child's life there can indeed be a natural dissociation between abilities of speech and abilities of mind. But if the burbler is told to struggle for precision, then a stammer entrenches itself and gets worse.

In later life one of the psychological explanations of stammering that seemed to make sense to me was that stammering is some sort of protection against the aggression of others; also against one's own potential aggression against them. That is – people can be disarmed by a stammer. But also, and perhaps more importantly, stammerers are people fighting against a natural tendency in themselves for confrontation, for doing other people down, for coming out on top.

However subtle this suggestion seemed in later life, the first part of it made no sense when I went to preparatory school at the age of nine. Here stammering was the opposite of a protection: the teasing of stammerers was one of the easiest of the rituals by which small boys tormented one another. A compensation however did seem to be that one learned that friendships could exist and indeed be enhanced through a lack of glibness with words.

At public school the teasing stopped, but painful embarrassments in classrooms did not. One judged one's happiness, almost one's health, on whether one's stammer was having a good day or a bad. Why could not teachers pass one over in the business of reciting or construing? However it seemed to be recognised both by oneself and by them that honour demanded that they should not.

During these years (the '30s and early '40s) I was sent to several
stammer therapists, but they seemed to concentrate on means of
soothing, or playing tricks on, a stammer, and not to look at what
might lie behind it. I remember demonstrations being given of how
I would not stammer if I spoke rhythmically and histrionically in the
manner of a politician or an actor or a clergyman – swooping and
pausing on the crests or in the troughs of waves. I was told of famous
politicians who had had a tendency to stammer – Aneurin Bevan,
even Winston Churchill. They had practised declamations in front
of a mirror, and look at them now! I was given speeches to practise
that rolled off my tongue in my therapist's consulting room; but when
I got outside this style seemed grotesque – and wrong on a deeper
level to that of stammering. If one stammered one simply suffered: if
one ranted or became mellifluous like a '30s politician, one seemed
in danger of losing one's soul.

When the time came for me to go into the army (this was 1942)
there was some doubt whether, because of my stammer, I would
be able to move together with my school contemporaries into the
training-groups earmarked to become officers. An infantry officer,
after all, has to make noises upon which lives and deaths depend. I
was warned that people seldom became officers who had stammers
as bad as mine. Looking back, it seems to me that the army authorities showed extraordinary sophistication with regard to my stammer.
They accepted me as an officer: I like to think their gamble paid
off; but it sometimes seemed touch and go.

During the early days of training when each cadet was taken out
in front of the squad to be in charge of the parade-ground drill, and
it sometimes seemed that I, standing hopefully with my mouth open,
might unwittingly become like the Emperor Christophe of Haiti who
used for his amusement to march his crack troops over a cliff. But then
mysteriously and in the nick of time orders did come out. I wondered
about this: if words came out in a crisis, why did they not come out
in ordinary life?

In the war, in which I was an infantry platoon commander in Italy,
I remember no occasion of any life-and-death importance when words
had any trouble in coming out. But there were times behind the lines
when I had to give lectures on such subjects as current affairs or regi-
mental history and then, again, there was the spectacle of myself like
an Aunt Sally at a fairground, and my audience being commanded
by my sergeant not to roll about in the aisles.

By the end of the war I had a good and successful platoon. Perhaps
we learned to trust each other. We all found ourselves from time to

time after all in positions like Aunt Sallys on a battleground.

After the war I was sent by the army to the best therapist I ever went to: he did not talk about evasions or anodynes; he talked about states of mind. Stammering was some condition of relationship with oneself: in speech a stammerer was too much on top of himself; he felt he had to be like other people who seemed to be at one with themselves; but if he could stand back from himself as it were, which might be more natural to him, then words might be freed to come out. I thought I saw what he meant about this: words except on rare occasions were so inadequate! To make sense, one usually wished to express two or more things at the same time. But it was true other people did not seem to feel like this. But if I came to be like them, would this always be like being involved in war? The therapist suggested – Perhaps you don't want to get rid of your stammer! I was amazed – me not want to get rid of my stammer? It was later that it was borne in on me more clearly that a stammer, a lack of glibness, might be an aid to good relationships and sensibility, as well as a curse and a protection.

I have continued to stammer, but the painful effects and embarrassment have gone, perhaps because as an adult I have been able to choose my own styles of life, or because I have continued to learn about compensations. I have had no temptations, that is, to become a politician or an actor or a clergyman. And I have been able to concentrate on being a writer without being asked to lecture, or do chat-shows, or take part in literary conferences. On the rare occasions in which I have performed publicly, on radio or television, I sometimes struggle somewhat and sometimes I do not: but I do not mind any more, and I hope this not minding is transmitted to an audience.

Over the years I have become fascinated by a person's use of words; by the relationship between what he is saying and what he is meaning and what is actually happening. Perhaps this is because I am a stammerer, or it may be that some original quirk of mind has caused both the stammer and the fascination. When I was young it seemed that in order to make sense so many things had to be said all at once! And of course this was complex. As a writer I have tried to look at questions such as – what is language trying to do: what are its falsities, what are its possibilities: what does my own experience mean when I can speak fluently in a crisis but often not otherwise? It seems that life-and-death communication is what language came into existence for – as a means of preserving oneself or the tribe. When humans settled down there was time for noises of less vital moment to be made: this was when language became more a matter of game-playing to pass the time – to cajole, to justify, to attack, to defend. But still, was there not yet a vital need for truth-telling; for enquiry? And was this not necessarily difficult? Anthropologists have found that when tribes settle they use language only seldom for communication; often its function is to preserve the identity of one's own group and to keep others out. There seems to be some connection here with the myth of the Tower of Babel: perhaps stammerers look back nostalgically to pre-Babel days when language (whatever this was) was used for learning, for building, for trying to get up to heaven. Meister Eckhart remarked – 'Whatever we say of things divine, we must stammer.'

It is striking how in all the modern developments of therapeutic techniques there is still no recognised 'cure' for stammering: the latest *Encyclopaedia Britannica* confesses 'stammering remains an enigma' and 'the possibility of some specific medical cure seems remote at the present time'. It seems to be recognised that stammering is to do with basic conundrums of human personality.

My own guess is that a stammerer is someone who from earliest days is alarmed at the power but also the oddities of words: here are all these grown-ups shouting, wheedling, arguing, performing: what on earth are they up to? Can they not hear how tenuous is the relationship between what they are saying and what is actually going on? A stammerer, I think, is someone who has a built-in tendency to hear himself; to glimpse the potential falsities of words. He can stand back from himself enough to see that if there is to be truth there is inevitably a problem, a struggle. What he cannot easily do (but has to learn how to try) is to take one step further back as it were so that he cannot only see the dangers in words but find an authority to deal with them.

But would this still depend on some form of stammering?

Adapted from *The Tatler*, 1984

From *Journey into the Dark,* VI

Voltaire famously said that if God did not exist it would be necessary to invent him. This remark has usually been taken to be ironic: to imply that such an invention would be an illusion. But when have human inventions been illusions? Inventions are the putting into practice of what has been discovered to exist; of realisations about how the world works. It might as well be said that if gravity did not exist it would be necessary to invent it – which in a sense is what Newton and Einstein did. Names are given to inventions and realisations and if they do not work they are forgotten. God is a name for the realisation that the world works in a certain way: that humans in relation to the world work in a certain way – both rationally in systems of cause-and-effect, and also apparently irrationally in systems in which a person's attitudes and choices seem to affect what is effected. How this can be experienced, put to good effect, is a matter of trial and error and trust. The trust seems to become feasible with the experience. The whole process remains partly in the dark.

It is simple to see the world in such a way as to find no evidence for God: humans have the freedom to choose their experiments; and reality, as scientists say, is a function of the experimental condition. Experimenters can choose meaningless determinism as a condition; and whatever it is that has influenced their choice can itself be seen as part of the chain of cause and effect – there need be no diversion from meaninglessness, if this is what is desired. Any inclination to step aside from determinism can be seen as an illusion; and the challenge – Well why not try a different experimental condition? – still leaves the decision to the person who confronts it.

However once there has been recognition of Wittgenstein's dictum – 'One thinks one is tracing the outline of a thing's nature and one is merely tracing round the frame through which we look at it' – then there is the challenge to become acquainted with the nature of frames, and by this to admit the possibility of the existence of what might be beyond them. The realisation that certain states by their nature seem to be essentially by-products – the experience of which cannot be directly summoned but which nevertheless through attention to other things can be known – this is an invitation to go on a journey. Wittgenstein suggested that once one had seen that in the normal course of reasoning one was tracing round frameworks, one could indeed go beyond these. To describe the condition required to make the journey valid he used another metaphor – One must throw away the ladder after one has climbed up on it.

The people who make a nonsense of the idea of God are not so much those who claim that the word refers to nothing – it can be reasonable to suppose that God does not exist – but rather those who claim exact knowledge of God and who thus describe him as if trapped within the frames of their spectacles. Religionists keep their God like a monkey on a string; they tell him what he can or cannot do; they use him to charm or frighten people into believing they should do what they are told; when they have bewitched their audiences they pass round the hat. But if one does not wish to stay at the stage of describing the frames of one's spectacles, making play with monkeys or tigers, then what is there to be said about God? Wittgenstein advocated silence. But he suggested there was still something to be heard in the so-called silence at the centre of the circumscription of words; and Wittgenstein in fact went on talking – about art, poetry, speculation. St Paul was a writer who seemed quite knowingly to be searching out, carving, his way in the dark: indeed not in silence but as if with the knowledge that what he found there would be a by-product of talking – meaning, beauty, recompense, salvation. St Paul is often accused of muddying a message that is essentially simple. Simple indeed! Only frameworks of spectacles are simple. Jesus made statements, offered descriptions, suggested injunctions, of which people could make what they liked. He said he would have to leave his followers or else they would not be able to see things as they were: they would always be seeing what they made of him through their spectacles. Once they were on their own they might have learned or be able to learn enough about frameworks to understand what he was and what he had been saying. This would be the equivalent of climbing a ladder and then throwing it away and embarking on a journey.

The state of grace is one in which you do not know exactly what is happening: you accept that you cannot know, you trust it will be all right. The framework of your spectacles is the circle of light within which you have been confined – by the conditioning of your past, of the society around you. But by acknowledging this you have become aware of what is beyond it. It may of course always seem easier to remain beneath the light. The saying that mankind cannot bear very much reality is a recognition that humans like staying within their circle; there they can argue, fight, justify, console – anything to distract them from what might be discovered in the dark. Once humans saw themselves as mad archaic statues striding forwards; then as bowed figures crushed beneath the weight of the sky; then as splintered fragments disappearing into space. (We have been at this corner of the garden before? well one returns to favourite art-works, does one not?) What we have never yet quite managed to see ourselves as are those grave and adoring faces looking down from the curve of a ceiling. But why not? This is the reality that it is difficult to bear to be part of – to have the circle of light above our head like a halo or a crown.

Without the invention or discovery of God humans have reasonably no responsibility; they are within the prison of the circle of light. But there is inexorably the impression that they have responsibility; and it is because of this that there is the call for the invention and the realisation of God. There is then the invitation to step into the dark: or perhaps there would never have been the invitation if there had not first been some ungainly step – a trip perhaps or a skip – in such a process time goes backwards and forwards as it does, so it is said, at the boundaries of space. God is that which is responsible for everything and nothing: a human is responsible for everything on earth and nothing: together, they are involved in ever more intricate steps, like dancing. The Holy Spirit is said to be that which has made love with a human: is not that the story? Well, a lot might happen if you throw away the ladder.

The effect of the recognition or the invention of God – the journey that you will be on when you have thrown away the ladder – is not that everything henceforth will be straightforward or that you will be given to know in advance what to do: it is rather that everything that happens or that you do will appear to be within the scheme of things; and that by being a participant in the present, you may have a hand in the pattern of future and past. What happens in the present changes not only one's view of the past but its nature: from such patterning there is also suggested a potential future. In a world without God there is no sensible attitude towards the past except complaint or justification: with these dominating the present they form the style of the future. Humans may feel they have autonomy without God, but how can they escape from the shackles of self-justification or resentment? There is no freedom in the present if there is no means of absolution from the past – nor indeed hope for a better future. God is that by which one realises things are worked out in time: of this there is no proof; an aesthetic aptitude is required to see patterns. But once seen, as with anything aesthetic, there they are. From self-justification or resentment nothing grows. But should one not have had, from the beginning, some knowledge of gardens?

And as for the evil and horror of this world – that which ravages and destroys living things and on account of which the idea of a good God is often said to be untenable – well at least, God knows, these cannot be said to be unexpected. Every myth, every pattern of understanding, takes cognisance of evil and horror; and often enough these happen under the eyes and even it seems under the hand of God. Myths struggle to understand and to come to terms with this: God is that by which use can be made of evil and horror, not that by which they will be prevented. Humans have the freedom to occasion evil and horror but also to fight them; and these are the conditions under which is recognised what is called life. If such conditions do not seem acceptable, all right! But there is the chance of learning: evil can be turned to use, and a change of pattern can be carried into the future – and these can seem like miracles. At what cost? Of course at some cost! There were snakes in God's garden.

Some of the essays earlier risked looking at the Holocaust – which people have said they find impossible to understand; concerning which some seem jealously to have guarded their right not to understand, for how much easier it is to say – How can God let this happen? And from this – How can there be a God! And voices out of shame or respect have had to be silent, who might say – It is since there is a God that there is outrage that these things happen, not that they don't happen: and since there thus is a God, humans might understand this and prevent them. In the Old Testament it is told how God from time to time threatened to obliterate his people; once or twice got to the brink of eliminating all living creatures. This was an early form of trying to come to terms with human outrage. Yet the time still does not quite seem to have come when humans can say – How can humans let this happen? and see that God is a means by which they might not. But this is the challenge – to see God as that which provides chances for evolution and learning, not that which takes such chances away. Evolution requires that there shall be cost and death; what has been learned is that humans have some ordering of these. God is that by which humans can see their predicaments and propensities; also that by which they can change.

Jews once saw themselves as people who, in his cosmic experiment, God had picked out to be representatives of the whole human race; those to whom God had given a special aptitude for knowing their earthly responsibility. Jews were conscious of their chance to participate in the scheme of things: but it would always be possible to turn away and say – It is God's fault for giving us this responsibility: we did not ask for it! But one says this only if one does not wish to learn how to handle it. If consciousness becomes too much of a burden – well indeed, this may be one outcome of the experiment. But Jews, and the human race, have survived – and with mixed success concerning responsibility.

It was when Jews seemed to feel that by being chosen for the experiment – by possessing the gift of some special aptitude of consciousness – they were not representative but set apart from the rest of the human species – not a nucleus but a separate cell – that something went awry: for if there was a nucleus that did not feel itself as a nucleus, then how was the experiment as a whole to proliferate and flourish? Jews, chosen by God – seeing themselves as chosen by God – began to be seen not only by others but by themselves as not representative but separate: and what might be the outcome of such a situation – of that being distinct which had been selected to represent the whole? There might indeed be the threat of annihilation all round; though still the chance to learn.

There have been other holocausts, other near-annihilations in history; none with such scope and ferocity; nor, with modern technology, such efficiency. The historical circumstances can be said to be exceptional – this can be accepted – but one significant circumstance is that the attempt to annihilate the Jews took place at a time when humanity seemed likely to be on the point of annihilating a large part of itself with the Bomb. What might stop them? What would be the cost! What realisation of their propensity for horror? There were lessons that everyone had to learn – and not just through the example of the Nazis' treatment of the Jews. But the human race survived. And Jews returned to their home. And others had to accept this. There had been so much horror! Still in the balance is the question whether, now they are home, Jews will eventually come to see themselves as a nucleus to humanity's cell, or whether they will continue to go their own way and not present a pattern of symbiosis from which everyone can learn. Circumstances are still such that a next annihilation may be of the whole human race.

It has been recognised by more than one pundit – notably by the prophet George Steiner – that it took a World War and indeed the Holocaust to provide the circumstances by which Jews could return home. The modern State of Israel had been dreamed of, planned, but it was born on the funeral-tails of humans' destructiveness and near self-destruction, and in the generally agreed hope that such events should not happen again. And so had some good come out of evil? But what had been learnt – what could still be learnt – about the idea that Jews might become – had been told by their prophets they might become – like a single cell invading and being assimilated by a larger cell: a seed or nucleus from which what had been learnt might spread – and now not only by means of suffering?

Christ was a Jew and his ministry was to Jews; what he seemed to teach was that humans had no separate homes – that their nature, able to be exemplified by Jews, was such that they should not be separate from the rest of the world but each and severally a nucleus. When at that time some two thousand years ago it became evident that because of history and tradition Jews did not wish to hear this message, it got blown about on the wind and landed upon gentiles' stony ground – stony, because what special aptitude did gentiles have for receiving and attending to this strange understanding – that they might each and severally become nuclei to a whole? Gentiles had been maintaining their identity for so long by fighting, justifying, envying, forming groups; how could they be alert to the chances of a relation-ship with a God who seemed to be offering them a partnership? And indeed with Jews now still seeing themselves as separate, whether as a nation or in scattered groups, how would their style be any differ-ent? This was the catastrophe – that Jews who seemed to have the aptitude for performing the function of a nucleus – of being alert to an evolutionary scheme of things with themselves at the centre – could not accept this, and became representative of the impression that such presumption was impossible; that more appropriate was a style of lamentation. And gentiles, picking up the seeds of what was to be called Christianity, heard the message of the need to become nuclei to the whole, but seemed to have little aptitude for handling it. From the seeds that they nurtured as it were in hothouse pots there grew sometimes exquisite but all too often obviously monstrous plants – the professions of peace and good will turning quite blatantly to virulence and savagery; professions to love both neighbours and enemies switch-ing gleefully to envy. All this had perhaps been foreseen; and indeed it was likely that such a cosmic experiment concerning freedom would have to go through many failures; grotesque dead-ends. How else is anything learned? And so long as there has been some learning, is there not the challenge to try again? At least on the part of individu-als, even if public efforts seem helpless. To love others as one loves oneself – the function of a symbiotic nucleus – indeed this is not easy or straightforward! In what manner, except as a by-product, can one worthily love oneself? But there it is – as an injunction. The life of a cell is dependent on its relationship not only with its nucleus and with the outside world, but with that higher ordering which has enabled it to know how things work. What is the reality, after all, that has set up, and maintains, the cosmic experimental condition?

The Christian myth ends, as so many good stories do, just at the point when something more interesting even than usual might have been elaborated – after the commandments, after the learning of the impossibility of wholly honouring these, after the promise of salvation through the recognition and enduring of this impossibility. But if one has a sense of no more than oneself, is not this latest requirement somewhat impossible too? A point had been reached at which it could reasonably be asked – Well what did, what does, happen then? Once there had been got over, that is, the scares and excitements about the end of the world and a second coming. Christians were told they had to choose: but how were they to choose rightly – once they had learned of the limitation of rules and obedience, but that, even if everything had been done for them, they still had everything to do? They were told to observe, to listen, to be attentive to what was going on around them, and by this they would be led into all truth. And this would not be the end of enquiry, but the beginning of a process. Their lack of an aptitude however for working with this guidance by the Spirit became all too soon apparent: how triumphantly they returned to their old love of complaint and aggression! how inexorable their demand for the sacrifice of others, not of themselves. And as for truth – should it not depend after all on those who had set themselves up as being in the know? How unintelligible was the Spirit! To love neighbours, enemies, as oneself – what did this mean? Had it not indeed been called gibberish? How much easier to try to sort things out by categorising, discriminating; even if this meant being at enmity even with those purporting to be on one's own side.

The world goes on its way much as it has done since the advent of consciousness, with humans fighting, arguing, doing one another down, and finding justifications for these proclivities. Humans in groups can only dream of something different, forward or back. But may not individuals hope to become nuclei within that larger whole that they sense is in travail, and at least dreams of change? Such an individual can be like a bicycle free-wheeler going down hill: a body-movement here, a touch on a handlebar there, and gravity is involved to occasion where you are going. And has it not been shown that insofar as it is through gravity that the world affects you, then it is through gravity, albeit infinitesimally, that you affect the world? Ah, the happy relativity of the station that moves in respect of the train! And nowadays there is the further elegant image of the butterfly in the rain-forest – that pregnant nucleus to an otherwise overwhelming world.

For someone trying to be in tune with this, who has felt at home with some such stammered ideas, for such a person the experience will not be primarily that of being swayed by, or paying much attention to, passions and prejudices; nor by reverently holding up in the light too simple systems of rationality and morals – even if these can be seen to be necessary and largely correct. It will be – but how absurdly simple, simply absurd, is the unsayable if one gets to saying it – the experience of knowing that just this or that has to be done. And how should one know this? Well, simply by means of everything one has ever been and ever done (We have been here before? You recognise the turning?); of everything unsayable that has already by others been said. Indeed there will be some darkness! But do you not now, having come this far, in fact understand this? How you have managed this – how you will come to affect things – perhaps you will never quite know. With your hands out, things are taken out of, put into, your hands. Hello, do I know you? There are indeed extraordinary coincidences – a meeting by a bandstand; a concatenation of stars. Who am I talking to? You. You thought we were walking in the garden? Isn't it time to throw away the ladder? God knows. But pull it up after you.

– Air tickets, travellers cheques, passport, health certificate. Probably not insurance.

Earlier it was suggested that literature seldom dealt with such situations. And now the philosopher Adorno has said there should be no more poetry after Auschwitz. At least no heroic lamentations.

So wave the children goodbye, old God, from the Garden, as they go.

Darwin said that he lost faith in God when he learned of the habits of the ichneumon wasp – the insect which plants its eggs in the paralysed body of a caterpillar so that its larvae can have fresh food as they grow. He did not say that he lost faith in nature: how could he? He was taking such pains to recognise it. But might he not have seen through it to – where – the loving thoughtfulness of wasp and caterpillar? Such parents! Lucky children.

Off you go then. Never mind the mess. You may not be able to send messages, but we'll know what you're up to.

Unpublished, 1998

LANNAN SELECTIONS

The Lannan Foundation, located in Santa Fe, New Mexico, is a family foundation whose funding focuses on special cultural projects and ideas which promote and protect cultural freedom, diversity, and creativity.

The literary aspect of Lannan's cultural program supports the creation and presentation of exceptional English-language literature and develops a wider audience for poetry, fiction, and nonfiction.

Since 1990, the Lannan Foundation has supported Dalkey Archive Press projects in a variety of ways, including monetary support for authors, audience development programs, and direct funding for the publication of the Press's books.

In the year 2000, the Lannan Selections Series was established to promote both organizations' commitment to the highest expressions of literary creativity. The Foundation supports the publication of this series of books each year, and works closely with the Press to ensure that these books will reach as many readers as possible and achieve a permanent place in literature. Authors whose works have been published as Lannan Selections include Ishmael Reed, Stanley Elkin, Ann Quin, Nicholas Mosley, William Eastlake, and David Antin, among others.

SELECTED DALKEY ARCHIVE PAPERBACKS

FOR A FULL LIST OF PUBLICATIONS, VISIT:
www.dalkeyarchive.com

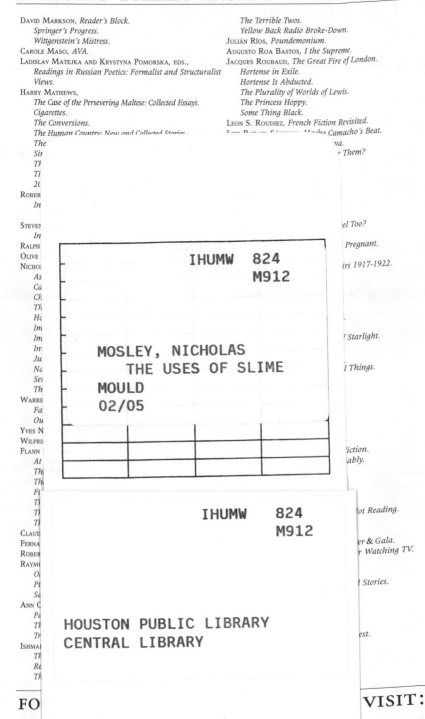

SELECTED DALKEY ARCHIVE PAPERBACKS

DAVID MARKSON, *Reader's Block.*
  Springer's Progress.
  Wittgenstein's Mistress.
CAROLE MASO, *AVA.*
LADISLAV MATEJKA AND KRYSTYNA POMORSKA, EDS.,
  *Readings in Russian Poetics: Formalist and Structuralist
  Views.*
HARRY MATHEWS,
  The Case of the Persevering Maltese: Collected Essays.
  Cigarettes.
  The Conversions.
  The Human Country: New and Collected Stories.
  The
  Sin
  Th
  Tl
  2(
ROBER
  In

STEVEN
  In
RALPH
OLIVE
NICHOL
  As
  Ca
  Ch
  Th
  Hc
  Im
  Im
  In
  Ju
  Na
  Se
  Th
WARRE
  Fa
  Ou
YVES N
WILFRII
FLANN
  At
  Th
  Th
  Pi
  Tl
  Tl
  Tl
CLAUD
FERNA
ROBER
RAYM(
  Oi
  Pi
  Sc
ANN (
  Pc
  Tl
  Tr
ISHMA
  Tl
  Re
  Th

The Terrible Twos.
  Yellow Back Radio Broke-Down.
JULIÁN RÍOS, *Poundemonium.*
AUGUSTO ROA BASTOS, *I the Supreme.*
JACQUES ROUBAUD, *The Great Fire of London.*
  Hortense in Exile.
  Hortense Is Abducted.
  The Plurality of Worlds of Lewis.
  The Princess Hoppy.
  Some Thing Black.
LEON S. ROUDIEZ, *French Fiction Revisited.*
Macho Camacho's Beat.
  va.
  r Them?

el Too?
Pregnant.
irs 1917-1922.

IHUMW 824
M912

Starlight.

MOSLEY, NICHOLAS
  THE USES OF SLIME
MOULD
02/05

Things.

fiction.
ably.

IHUMW 824
M912

lot Reading.

er & Gala.
r Watching TV.

Stories.

HOUSTON PUBLIC LIBRARY
CENTRAL LIBRARY

est.

FO

VISIT: